GUMBO SHOP®

TRADITIONAL AND CONTEMPORARY CREOLE CUISINE

A NEW ORLEANS
RESTAURANT COOKBOOK

BY RICHARD STEWART

FOREWORD BY PEGGY SCOTT LABORDE

Text and Recipes: Richard Stewart
Foreword: Peggy Scott Laborde
Design: Michael Ledet Art & Design
Photography: Neil Greentree
Food and Photo Styling: Michael Ledet and Richard Stewart
Editing: Mimi Byrnes Pelton
Typography: Eugenie S. Delaney

Library of Congress Cataloging-in-Publication Data available

ISBN 0-9668636-0-7

First Edition
Fifth Printing

Gumbo Shop®
5900 South Front Street
New Orleans, LA 70115
www.gumboshop.com
Printed in Korea

ACKNOWLEDGMENTS

It's amazing how many people it takes to produce a cookbook.

Thanks to:

Allain Bush of Bush Antiques, Eddie Dodge of Dodge Fjeld Antiques, Dindy Stewart, Fred Davis and Mary Stewart for china, flatware, tablecloths and other photographic props.

Cynthia Martin and Candace Cox for invaluable help and patience in testing recipes.

Guy Pellitteri for much assistance in writing the wine and cocktail sections.

Bill Roberts for his support throughout this project.

Baxter and Britton Stewart for their encouragement.

Susan LeBlanc and Vicki Lopez for holding my calls and Joan Levy for paying the bills.

Stan Melancon for hosting Neil, the photographer, and for lots of chauffeuring.

Eddie Finkelstein for watching my car.

All 67 Gumbo Shop employees for making this a possibility.

The 250,000 customers who each year eat some Gumbo Shop food.

Countless other friends, relatives, business associates, acquaintances, neighbors, strangers, and others who lent their valuable observations, critiques, words of support, advice and sometimes pointless, but humorous, comments along the way.

December 2, 1998
New Orleans, Louisiana

RICHARD STEWART, a native and life long resident of New Orleans is the President and Executive Chef of Gumbo Shop. He is a graduate of the University of New Orleans School of Hotel, Restaurant and Tourism Administration, a member of the American Culinary Federation, and serves as Vice President of French Quarter Festivals, Inc. He has taught courses in Louisiana Cooking, authored food and culture articles for several local publications, and this is his first cookbook.

PEGGY SCOTT LABORDE, also a native of the city, works as a producer for WYES, the New Orleans PBS affiliate, and is well known as a knowledgeable and reliable local cultural pundit. Among her many credentials are ten documentaries including "Mardi Gras: The Passing Parade," "New Orleans in the Sixties" and "A Holy New Orleans!" Peggy is a founding board member of the Tennessee Williams/New Orleans Literary Festival. This is Peggy's first contribution to a cookbook.

MICHAEL LEDET, another native and life long local resident is a professional artist, graphic designer and educator. He is on the faculty of Loyola University, and, as a graphic artist, specializes in arts and history publications for such clients as the New Orleans Arts Council and the prestigious Historic New Orleans Collection. Michael's drawings and paintings are collected and shown from coast to coast. This is his first cookbook.

NEIL GREENTREE is a native Australian who currently resides in Washington D. C. He is employed by the Smithsonian Institute where his duties include documenting Indian temples and other Asian art. His freelance works range from gourmet food catalogues to restaurant publicity shots. This is Neil's first cookbook.

MIMI BYRNES PELTON is a native New Orleanian who left her home as a bride. She has taken her hospitality and food heritage with her wherever she's lived and has served gumbos, jambalaya and red beans to friends in Oregon, Texas, Illinois, Virginia and Rhode Island. After a career in educational publication, she is back home in New Orleans, writing, editing, and, especially, cooking.

EUGENIE S. DELANEY is a native New Orleanian who now lives in North Ferrisburgh, Vermont with her husband, Michael and daughter, Madeline. She has been designing and producing books for over 14 years.

CONTENTS

FOREWORD

New Orleans is a Mecca of culinary temptations and as a native I wouldn't want it any other way. Temptation and atonement are part of our culture. With religious roots that are primarily Catholic, thanks to our French founders, the church affects our calendar in a rather unique way: we celebrate Mardi Gras, or Fat Tuesday, the final day of feasting before 40 days of Lent. The traditional abstinence from meat during this time leading up to Easter means that we have to "sacrifice" by enjoying the bounty from nearby waters: fish, shrimp and oysters from the Gulf of Mexico, crabs from Lake Pontchartrain; and crawfish from area swamplands.

New Orleans was founded by the French in 1718 and named after the regent, the Duke D'Orleans. Passed to the Spanish for a while, it went back to France long enough for Napoleon to sell it to a fledgling United States of America in 1803.

In New Orleans, the French influence over local cooking was just the beginning. Throughout the years African slaves were often the cooks. Through one of the nation's busiest ports have come new citizens from Germany, Ireland, the French Caribbean Islands, Italy and Greece, Croatia and, more recently, Asia. The Choctaw Indians were already living in this swampy mosquito-infested piece of land, below sea level and shaped like a crescent on the Mississippi River. They introduced powdered sassafras or filé which they called "kombo" to settlers as a staple for one of many styles of the indigenous soup we call gumbo, from the African word "kingumbo" meaning the vegetable okra. A gumbo usually contains either filé or okra as a thickener. Just as gumbo is a blend of many cultures, so is the origin of the word. However, the base of most gumbos is "roux" — flour and fat with seasonings that is browned to provide an almost nutty flavor.

Defining New Orleans cooking are the terms "Creole" and "Cajun." A word whose meaning has been transformed over the years, "Creole" generally refers to anything native to New Orleans. Traditionally it described a person of French and Spanish roots born in the colonies. Recently it has come to also include African in that mix. When referring to food, it refers to more sophisticated city cooking typical of New Orleans.

"Cajun" describes cooking from Southwestern Louisiana — the legacy of the Acadians, descendants of French Canadian communities in Nova Scotia and New Brunswick expelled by the British in the middle 1700's. Rich, hearty and often spicy are the characteristics of Cajun cooking. With other ethnic influences playing a part in both types of cooking, the lines separating these two culinary styles have become as fuzzy as the outer skin of the green spindly okra.

The Gumbo Shop is located in one of America's most historic neighborhoods — the "Vieux Carre" (French for "old square"), also known as the French Quarter. Open since the 1920's as a restaurant, according to veteran New Orleans architect Henry Krotzer, this Louisiana Colonial townhouse at 630 St. Peter Street is one of a handful of 18th Century buildings left in the Quarter.

The structure was built in 1795 to replace a building that was destroyed in the devastating 1794 fire that started around the corner from the restaurant and almost wiped out the city. There was a commercial establishment downstairs and a residence above, typical of land use at that time. Among its more illustrious inhabitants was John Watkins, who was Mayor of New Orleans in the early 1800's. The ground floor of the 200 year-old building was once a woodworking shop.

The carriageway entry to the Gumbo Shop leads you to either an inviting tropical courtyard under a canopy of banana trees or a quaint interior lined with murals in warm gold-brown tones depicting scenes from New Orleans' past. Painted on the burlap wrappings of cotton bales in 1925 by local artist Marc Antony, the scenes are of the restaurant's neighbors, the Presbytere and the Cabildo — the earliest seats of government and the site of the Louisiana Purchase.

Mrs. Margaret Popora ran the restaurant from the 1940's until she sold the business to Bill Roberts in 1977. Richard Stewart operates the business and, with his staff, has compiled the recipes in this book.

Above the ground floor of the Gumbo Shop building you could easily expect to find Stanley Kowalksi and his spouse, Stella. Not too far fetched when you learn that Tennessee Williams, who

considered New Orleans his spiritual home, completed his Pulitzer Prize winning play, "A Streetcar Named Desire" while living in an apartment on the top floor of a building next door at 632 St. Peter. From the windows of his apartment he could see "that rattletrap old streetcar" named Desire whose route included nearby Royal Street and Bourbon Street.

Just a half-block away towards the Mississippi River is Jackson Square, named for Andrew Jackson, the hero of the Battle of New Orleans who later became President of the United States. With the St. Louis Cathedral right in the center of the Square, "those Cathedral bells" that the tragic Blanche duBois referred to in "Streetcar" can be heard in the restaurant's courtyard, further contributing to the fact that the Gumbo Shop is at ground zero when it comes to a quintessential New Orleans experience. This is a place that could easily slip by on ambiance alone.

But that's not the Gumbo Shop's way.

The Tennessee Williams/New Orleans Literary Festival, held each Spring, takes place four doors away from the restaurant at Le Petit Theatre. Every year there's a "Stella and Stanley" shouting contest. Since the contest's beginning, one of many ways the restaurant connects to locals as well as visitors is to offer a prize of dinner at Gumbo Shop. One of their always creative newspaper ads has a tee shirted hunk yelling, "Stella — I want my gumbo!"

And there's a reason why the t-shirt was a regular part of the Kowalski wardrobe. In New Orleans it gets hot. To find dishes like hearty gumbo and heavy red beans a traditional staple may seem odd, but we do have our sub-tropical climate to thank for the vegetables that also make up

our diet. In addition to the outside heat, it is also reflected in the way our food tastes. We aren't shy with our use of pepper.

As a native New Orleanian, one of my duties is to answer the eternal question from visitors who cross my path. Where to eat? For value, quality and convenience, consistently at the top of my list has been the Gumbo Shop. With the French Quarter as the city's main attraction, the patrons of many eateries there are visitors.

At the Gumbo Shop, there's a welcome balance of locals as well.

And now, with the cookbook, you can create a taste of New Orleans in your own home, Gumbo Shop style. You don't even have to yell "Stella!" to prepare a "stellar" meal.

— *Peggy Scott Laborde*

INTRODUCTION

There's really nothing new in this cookbook. While all the recipes contain nuances of preparation or special ingredients that may be unique to Gumbo Shop, they all simply represent our versions of local standards, many going back to the days of French speaking cooks and French Market fish mongers — days that to many New Orleanians do not seem that long ago. It's been said that in the South the past isn't dead, and in New Orleans the past isn't even past. Generations of changing culinary trends, evolving tastes and increasingly sophisticated palates notwithstanding, local people *still* cook and eat and discuss these dishes with great gusto. While the Gumbo Shop menu is billed as offering "traditional and contemporary Creole cuisine," year after year our biggest sellers tend toward the traditional. Evolving naturally as a reflection of our culture, these foods retain their soulful and satisfying quality.

RESTAURANT COOKING VS. HOME COOKING

We cook gumbo in 125 gallon batches and make roux with 20 gallons of oil and 200 pounds of flour. Besides volume, there are other differences in how food is prepared in a restaurant compared to a home kitchen. Ingredients are not measured by volume but weighed in pounds and hundredths of pounds. Spices are measured in grams. Stocks are standardized with rigidly specified ingredients, cooking times and temperature. Often equipment is designed and built to best produce a specific dish. Cooking methods are developed to maintain consistency from batch to batch, day to day, cook to cook. And, of course, the importance of sanitation is paramount.

All the recipes in this book have been derived from the actual ones used in our restaurant and catering operations, and prepared as directed, should closely, if not exactly, replicate the dishes just as we serve them. As some ingredients may vary in flavor or quality, the result may vary somewhat. But Creole food is a forgiving cuisine, with so many parts contributing to the whole, that a delicious dinner is most likely certain.

USING THIS BOOK

The recipes begin with a chapter on gumbo, of course, and, as the universal Louisiana food, we suggest reading several of these before preparing any of the dishes. You will find several structures and methods that repeat themselves, giving you a good overview of Creole food. One method mentioned is the process of "sticking and scraping," in which sautéed seasoning vegetables and tomatoes are allowed to stick to the bottom of the pot to a point just short of burning, then scraped up and mixed back into the rest of the contents. Repeated several times in the beginning stages of a gumbo or Creole sauce, a depth of flavor unfolds that cannot be achieved otherwise.

Also, be sure to read the section immediately following this introduction entitled "First You Make a Roux." Since a roux is the backbone of so many dishes, you should become comfortable with the process before risking an investment in shrimp, crawfish or other ingredients. To make things as foolproof as possible, photographs of a light roux and a dark roux have been included.

Besides chapters on entrees, beans and rice, po-boys and desserts, we have added a "lagniappe" section with recipes for favorite Gumbo Shop cocktails. The book seemed incomplete without them considering, the city's "joie de vivre". In fact, according to some historians the term "cocktail" owes its origin to Antoine Peychaud who served his original Sazerac in a *coquetier* or "egg cup" shortly after settling in New Orleans.

CREOLE FOOD AND WINE

For years it was commonly quipped in New Orleans that our favorite white wine was gin and the favorite red wine was bourbon. In the scope of our history this seems odd, considering that the French, Spanish and Italians all hail from wine loving countries. Wine cellars were found in many old Creole homes, and the city's grand restaurants always featured respectable wine lists. However, it wasn't until the 1980's that a widespread appreciation of wine began to emerge in the city, and our food loving locals took to the trend with abandon. Over the last seven years the "New Orleans Wine and Food Experience," held every summer, has grown into a nationally recognized event.

At Gumbo Shop we have recognized the natural affinity of everyday Creole foods and fine wine for years. In general, fruity wines with smooth tannins match up well with bold assertive flavors such as tomato based sauces and heavily spiced dishes, while wines with high acidity like some Sauvignon Blancs and French styled Chardonnays match up well with foods that have rich creamy sauces and subtle flavors. California style oak aged Chardonnays , which are usually oak aged and undergo malolactic fermentation, are better suited to grilled or blackened fish and chicken.

As a mixture of many ingredients and with a rich tapestry of flavors, most traditional Creole dishes work well with a variety of wines. Chicken Andouille Gumbo, with its deep but delicate flavor, hearty stock and smokey sausage stands up to a big Cabernet Sauvignon, yet is nicely complimented by a classy Pinot Noir or an elegant Chardonnay. It is hard to go too far wrong — just try your favorite wines and see how they play against different aspects of these dishes. We change our list seasonally, always experimenting with the seemingly infinite number of fine wines available these days.

FIRST YOU MAKE A ROUX

To a seasoned local, the phrase "first you make a roux" clearly and succinctly communicates a common beginning to a recipe. "Light or dark" or "oil or butter" would be the only appropriate question, and in the context of the recipe, even that would likely be unnecessary. But to the uninitiated, the task seems to require great culinary skill, maybe some specialized cooking utensils, and perhaps a basic grasp of the French language.

Simply stated, roux is nothing more than flour cooked in some sort of fat. For most Creole and Cajun cooking the fat is vegetable oil (peanut oil,

soybean oil) and the flour is cooked to varying shades of brown. The recipes in this book call for either a light "peanut butter colored" roux, or a dark roux, about the color of chocolate.

Here's the procedure: Use a heavy bottomed pan such as black iron, enamel clad iron, or good quality stainless steel with a slab of aluminum fused to the bottom of the pot. The pot should be large enough to be easily and thoroughly stirred with a wire whip, and to accommodate the rest of the ingredients called for in the recipe.

Place the oil in the pot and set it over a medium high heat. Whisk in the flour, making sure it is evenly blended and free of lumps. Continue stirring as the roux cooks and bubbles. The bubbles are an indication that moisture is being boiled out of the flour. As soon as the bubbling stops and the aroma becomes similar to popcorn, the flour is actually frying, and the rate of browning accelerates rapidly. In other words, pay very close attention from this point on.

Stir constantly, and as soon as the proper color is attained, carefully add the seasoning vegetables. The addition of room temperature ingredients will immediately lower the temperature of the roux and, halting the browning process, will prevent the roux from burning. Also, the natural sugars contained in onions added at this time will immediately start to caramelize, releasing a wonderful savory flavor. After adding the seasoning vegetables, reduce the heat a bit and proceed with the rest of the recipe.

Most gumbo recipes call for a dark roux, rendering a deep color and nutty flavor. A lighter roux works better for sauces, because the less flour is cooked, the more thickening power it maintains. And remember, burned roux tastes awful and cannot be salvaged. Throw it out and start over. One way to quickly master roux making is to cook one sacrificial roux — keep cooking and stirring until it actually does burn. You will witness all the stages of the process, and any 'roux making fear' will dissolve.

One more note — be careful! Splattering roux can cause painful burns.

— Richard Stewart

GUMBO AND SOUP

Although it would seem to be a cold weather dish, gumbo is consumed year round in New Orleans. The variations on this hearty soup with African roots, that has either filé (powdered sassafras) or okra as a thickener, can include seafood or poultry and sausage or even a multitude of greens. One thing all these types of gumbo have in common is that they are served over rice, a major Louisiana crop. While gumbo is often served as a main dish, it's also used as an appetizer. Either way, gumbo is usually the soup du jour for most Louisianians.

— PSL

The perennial best seller at the restaurant, this gumbo is a summertime favorite in New Orleans. Though our Cajun cousins may balk at the idea of eating a hot bowl of gumbo in July's searing heat, it is the time when all the essential ingredients are fresh and abundant — blue crabs, gulf shrimp, fresh okra and meaty Creole tomatoes.

We have "de-seasonalized" the recipe, allowing the convenience of frozen okra and canned tomatoes, and since shrimp are one of the few seafood items not to suffer much when properly frozen, this dish can be enjoyed year round.

SEAFOOD OKRA GUMBO
Serves 6 to 8

2 lbs. fresh or frozen shrimp, head on about 40-50 count per lb.	1 cup chopped green bell pepper
2 small blue crabs, cleaned, fresh or frozen	½ cup chopped celery
3 quarts water	2 tsp. minced garlic
2 Tbls. cooking oil	1 16 ounce can chopped tomatoes
1 quart fresh or frozen okra, sliced into ½-inch rounds	2 bay leaves
⅔ cup cooking oil	2 tsp. salt (or to taste)
½ cup all purpose flour	½ tsp. black pepper
2 cups chopped onions	½ tsp. white pepper
	¼ tsp. cayenne pepper

Peel and de-vein the shrimp, and set aside, covered, in the refrigerator. Rinse the shrimp shells and heads, place in a non-reactive stock pot along with 2 quarts of water. Bring to a boil, reduce heat and simmer for 30 to 45 minutes to make a stock. Strain, discard the shells and heads and set the stock aside. Meanwhile, wash the crabs well under running water, place in a non-reactive pot with 1 quart of water, bring to a boil and simmer for 20 to 30 minutes. Strain, reserving stock and crabs. When the crabs are cool enough to handle, snap both claws off then break the body in half. Set aside.

In a heavy bottomed skillet, heat 2 tablespoons of oil , add the okra and sauté over medium high heat for about 10 to 15 minutes or until all the "ropiness" is gone. This step may take a little longer if fresh okra is used. Frozen vegetables are usually plunged into boiling water and blanched before freezing, so they are partially cooked.

Place the ⅔ cup oil in a large (8 quart) heavy bottomed non-reactive

(continued on page 16)

Dutch oven type pot. Add the flour and, over a medium high heat, make a dark brown roux. (See roux photo, page 10) As soon as the proper color is achieved, add the onions, bell pepper, celery, and garlic. Sauté, stirring occasionally until tender. During this process, allow the vegetables to stick to the bottom of the pan a bit, then scrape the bottom with a metal spoon or spatula. This allows some of the natural sugars in the onions to caramelize, rendering great depth of flavor.

When the seasoning vegetables are tender add the tomatoes, bay leaves, the three peppers and the salt. Cook for about 10 minutes, repeating the stick and scrape process with the tomatoes. Add the sautéed okra and cook for 10 more minutes.

Add the crab stock and half of the shrimp stock to the pot. Stirring constantly, bring the pot to a boil. Lower the heat a bit, partially cover and simmer for about one hour, stirring occasionally. If the gumbo appears too thick, add more stock to adjust. Add salt to taste and adjust the pepper if desired. Add the broken crabs and simmer for about 10 minutes. Add the peeled shrimp, return to a boil and simmer until the shrimp are firm and pink, about 5 minutes. Remove the pot from heat.

As is the case with most gumbos, this dish is best prepared either early in the day it is to be served, or even the day before, thereby allowing time for the flavors to marry. When reheating, stir often and be careful to avoid overcooking the shrimp.

Serve in large bowls over steamed rice.

CHICKEN ANDOUILLE GUMBO

Serves 8 to 10

1	chicken, 2-2½ lbs.	¾	pound Andouille sausage,
3	quarts water		sliced into ¼-inch rounds
1	lb. fresh or frozen okra, sliced	1	bay leaf
	into ½-inch rounds	1	tsp. thyme
½	cup plus 2 Tbls. cooking oil	1	tsp. basil
½	cup all purpose flour	½	tsp. sage
2	cups chopped onions	½	tsp. black pepper
1	cup chopped green bell	½	tsp. white pepper
	pepper	¼	tsp. cayenne pepper
½	cup chopped celery	2	tsp. salt
1	16 ounce can chopped		
	tomatoes		

A regional fusion dish, this gumbo features elements of both Creole and Cajun cooking traditions. The okra and tomatoes of New Orleans style gumbos mingle with smoky Andouille sausage from Cajun country for this Louisiana hybrid.

Cut chicken into eight pieces, cover with water and simmer for about one hour until chicken is tender and easily removed from the bones. Pour off stock and set aside. Allow chicken to cool, remove from bones and set aside.

In a large heavy skillet sauté the okra in 2 tablespoons oil for about 10 to 15 minutes or until all "ropiness" is gone. Set aside.

Meanwhile, in a large heavy bottomed Dutch oven, heat ½ cup oil over medium high heat. Add the flour and make a dark brown roux. (See roux photo, page 10). As soon as the proper color is achieved, add the onions, bell pepper and celery and sauté, stirring occasionally until tender. During this process, allow the vegetables to stick to the bottom of the pan a bit, then scrape the bottom with a metal spoon or spatula. This allows some of the natural sugars in the onions to caramelize, rendering great depth of flavor.

When the vegetables are tender, add the tomatoes, Andouille sausage and

(continued on next page)

sautéed okra. Continue cooking and stirring for about 15 minutes. Add the bay leaf, thyme, basil, sage, peppers and salt and mix well. Pour in about 8 cups of the chicken stock, bring to a slow boil, lower the heat and simmer for 1 hour, stirring occasionally. Add the cooked chicken and additional stock if necessary and simmer for 15 more minutes. Adjust seasoning and serve in large bowls over steamed rice.

SMOKED DUCK AND OYSTER GUMBO

Serves 8 to 10

1	duckling, about 3 lbs.	1	tsp. thyme
2½	quarts water	½	tsp. basil
½	cup butter	½	tsp. sage
½	cup flour	1	tsp. black pepper
1½	cups chopped onion	½	tsp. white pepper
1½	cups chopped green bell pepper	½	tsp. cayenne pepper
1½	cups chopped celery	2	tsp. salt
1	Tbls. minced garlic	1	cup chopped tomatoes, fresh or canned
1	Tbls. filé powder	2	cups oysters and their liquor
1	bay leaf		

Combining oysters with any poultry always makes for a happy marriage, but coupling the bivalves with the deep rich flavor of smoked duck renders a match made in heaven. This recipe takes some time, and it is best to start a day or two before you plan to serve it.

Using a backyard smoker or covered barbecue grill, smoke the duckling until done, following the smoker or grill manufacturer's directions. When cool enough to handle, remove the skin and set aside. Remove all the meat, cut the breasts and any large pieces into bite sized chunks and set aside, covered, in the refrigerator.

Heat oven to 400°. Arrange the duck skin on a shallow roasting pan and roast until it is crisp and the fat is rendered, about 20 minutes. Drain off fat and reserve.

Place the duck bones, duck skin and water in a stock pot. Bring to a boil, reduce the heat and simmer, partially covered, for 4 hours. Strain the stock and allow it to cool, then skim off the excess fat from the top. This is best done the day before, then refrigerated overnight so the solidified fat can be easily lifted off.

In a large heavy bottomed Dutch oven, melt the butter over a medium high heat. Whisk in the flour and make a dark brown roux. (See roux photo, page 10).

(continued on page 21)

As soon as the roux is the correct color, add the onion, bell pepper, celery and a tablespoon of the rendered duck fat. Cook until the vegetables are tender, stirring and scraping the bottom of the pan every few minutes. Add the filé, the spices and the chopped tomatoes and cook for 5 more minutes, stirring and scraping.

Stir in 6 cups of the stock, mix well and bring to a boil. Lower the heat and simmer for 20 minutes. Adjust the seasoning and add a little more stock if the gumbo is too thick. Add the reserved duck meat, return to a boil and simmer for 15 minutes. Add the oysters and cook just until their edges are curled, about 5 minutes. Remove the pot from the heat and serve in large bowls over steamed rice.

TURKEY AND HOT SAUSAGE GUMBO

Serves 8 to 10

M ake this gumbo on the weekend after Thanksgiving. It's
tastier than most other recipes for
leftovers, and soothing after a
rigorous day of Christmas shopping.
The hot sausage called for is
Chaurice — a peppery fresh (not
smoked) sausage of Spanish origin.

In the early 18th century,
families from the Spanish Canary
Islands settled in what is now St.
Bernard Parish, where their proud
descendents, known as "Isleños,"
carry on many ancestral traditions.

1½	lbs. cooked turkey meat	2	bay leaves
1	turkey carcass	1	tsp. thyme
1	lb. Chaurice sausage or other fresh hot link sausage	½	tsp. basil
¾	cup butter	½	tsp. sage
½	cup flour	½	tsp. white pepper
1	cup chopped onion	½	tsp. black pepper
1	cup chopped green bell peppers	¼	tsp. cayenne pepper
1	cup chopped celery	2	tsp. salt
1	Tbls. minced garlic	2	cups diced tomatoes, fresh or canned
1	Tbls. filé powder	2	quarts turkey stock

Trim as much meat as possible from the turkey carcass and cut about 1½ pounds of meat into bite sized pieces. Set aside. Break the turkey carcass into several pieces and place in a stock pot with 3 quarts of water. Bring the pot to a boil, lower the heat and simmer for 3 to 4 hours. Strain the stock and set aside.

Meanwhile, slice the hot sausage into ½-inch rounds and spread out evenly on a sheet pan or shallow baking pan. Place in a hot oven (400°) and allow the sausage to brown, about 20 minutes. Carefully remove the pan from the oven and pour off the rendered fat. Set the sausage aside.

In a large heavy bottomed Dutch oven, melt the butter over a medium high heat. (If you wish you may replace part or all of the butter with the rendered sausage fat). Whisk in the flour and make a dark brown roux. (See roux photo, page 10) As soon as it is the proper color add the chopped onion, bell pepper and celery. Stir well and cook until tender, from time to time allowing the vegetables to stick a bit and then scraping up the bottom of the pan.

Add the garlic and cook for 1 minute. Stir in the bay leaves, thyme, basil, sage, white, black and cayenne pepper and salt. Cook for 1 minute. Add the chopped tomatoes and cook for 5 minutes, repeating the sticking and scraping process.

Slowly pour in the turkey stock, mixing well. Bring the pot to a boil, reduce the heat and simmer for 30 minutes. Add the reserved turkey meat and sliced cooked sausage and bring back to a boil. Lower the fire and simmer for 15 minutes. Adjust the seasoning, skim off any excess fat and add a little more stock if the gumbo is too thick. Serve in large bowls over steamed rice.

Gumbo Z'herbes

Serves 20

It is no secret that New Orleanians like to celebrate. Any event will do, even a somber funeral or a tragic Saints football game. This custom goes way back, to when this predominately Catholic town's early cooks found a way to celebrate the penitential abstinence and fasting of lent.

Gumbo Z'herbes (from the French "aux herbes," meaning with herbs, or greens), and sometimes referred to as Gumbo Verte (Green Gumbo), is in structure the same as other gumbos, with a variety of fresh greens replacing the poultry, pork or seafood. Our updated version includes chopped smoked mushrooms for depth of flavor and red kidney beans for substance. Served over rice, Gumbo Z'herbes is delicious, nutritious and satisfying.

1	cup olive oil
1	cup flour
2	cups chopped onions
1	cup chopped bell pepper
¾	cup chopped celery
¾	cup minced shallots
¼	cup minced garlic
6	bay leaves
1½	tsp. thyme
1½	tsp. black pepper
2	tsp. white pepper
¾	tsp. cayenne pepper
2	Tbls. salt
1	lb. mushrooms, smoked (see Note, page 26)
1	gallon water
1	bunch collard greens
1	small head cabbage
1	bunch turnip greens, chopped
1	bunch mustard greens, chopped
1	bunch green onions
¼	cup chopped parsley
1	Tbls. soy sauce
1	lb. red beans, cooked

In a large heavy bottomed pot, heat the olive oil over a medium high heat. Add the flour and stir until a peanut butter colored roux is attained. (See roux photo, page 10) Immediately add the onion, bell pepper and celery. Sauté until vegetables are tender and start to stick and brown a little. Add the shallots, garlic, herbs, salt and peppers. Cook for 5 minutes, stirring often.

Meanwhile, in a large soup pot, bring the water (and bean water — see Note, page 26) to a boil. Chop the collards and cabbage into one inch squares and boil until just tender. Add the turnip greens, mustard greens and green onions and return to a boil. A 10 ounce package of frozen greens may be substituted for any of the fresh greens.

Coarsely chop the smoked mushrooms. Add it to the roux mixture and cook for 2 minutes. Carefully stir the roux-vegetable-mushroom mixture into

(continued on page 26)

Local folklore has it that you must make Gumbo Z'herbes with an odd number of greens, and what ever the number of greens in the gumbo eaten on Good Friday, that is the number of new friends you will make during the following year. Another version holds that a Holy Thursday supper of Gumbo Z'herbes containing seven greens, followed by chance meetings of seven people on Good Friday, blesses the fortunate diner with good luck all year.

the simmering greens, and return to a boil. Add the parsley, cooked red beans, and soy sauce to taste.

Bring to a boil one more time, then turn off the fire. Serve over rice.

This dish is best if refrigerated over night then reheated. This recipe yields about two gallons of gumbo. Freeze some for emergency penance!

Note: To smoke mushrooms, wash one pound of medium sized mushrooms, trim the bottom of the stems, and place on a pan in a smoker for about 45 minutes.

To cook red beans, rinse and sort 1 pound of red beans, cover with water and soak over night. Simmer over a low fire for 1 to 2 hours, until just tender. Drain, reserving the water to use as part of the water for cooking the greens.

In a pinch, you may use canned beans (two 15 ounce cans), drained and rinsed well.

FILÉ GUMBO

Serves 6 to 8

1	chicken, about 2½ lbs.	¾	lb. smoked sausage, sliced
3	quarts water		into ¼-inch rounds
½	cup plus 2 Tbls. butter	2	tsp. salt
2	cups chopped onion	½	tsp. black pepper
2	cups chopped green bell	½	tsp. white pepper
	pepper	¼	tsp. cayenne pepper
2	cups chopped celery	2	cups tomato sauce
¼	cup minced garlic	¼	tsp. Tabasco sauce
¼	cup filé powder		

Cut the chicken into eight pieces and place it in a stock pot. Cover with 3 quarts water, bring to a boil, lower heat and simmer for about 1 hour until tender and easily removed from the bones. Remove the chicken from the pot and when cool enough to handle separate the skin and bones from the meat. Cut the meat into bite sized pieces and set aside. Strain the stock, let it settle awhile, and skim the excess fat from the top. Set it aside for later use.

In a large heavy bottomed Dutch oven melt the butter over a medium heat. Add the onion, celery and bell pepper and sauté until tender, allowing the vegetables to stick and brown a bit during the process. Add the chopped garlic and cook 2 minutes. Stir in the filé and sauté, stirring often, for 5 minutes. Add the smoked sausage, salt, and three peppers and cook for 10 minutes. Add the tomato sauce and Tabasco. Cook for about 10 minutes, allowing it to stick a bit and scraping the bottom of the pan often.

Slowly add 8 cups of the chicken stock, stirring continually. Bring the pot to a boil and simmer for 20 minutes. Adjust the seasoning and add more stock if the gumbo appears too thick or spicy. Add the cooked chicken meat and simmer for 10 more minutes. Remove the pot from the heat and serve over steamed rice.

Having established that New Orleans is not a Cajun city, and that our roots and culinary traditions are Creole, let's now introduce this popular Cajun gumbo we often serve. Note that it does not contain roux or okra.

Filé, a powder ground from leaves of the sassafras tree, was adopted from the native Choctaw Indians and used by the Cajuns as a flavoring and thickening agent.

OYSTER AND ARTICHOKE SOUP

Serves 5 to 6

T*he Spanish brought the arti-*
choke to Louisiana, but it was
not until the latter half of the 20th
century that it was wedded with
our local oysters for this Creole
creation. Using fresh artichokes
renders a truly luxurious dish, but
if they are unavailable or if time is
an issue, canned artichoke hearts
work well, too.

4	large or 6 medium artichokes	½	tsp. sage
	-or-	½	tsp. thyme
1	cup drained and well rinsed	½	tsp. black pepper
	canned artichoke hearts	½	tsp. white pepper
½	cup butter	¼	tsp. cayenne pepper
1½	cup finely chopped onion	1½	tsp. salt
½	cup finely chopped celery	⅓	cup flour
½	cup finely chopped green bell	1½	cups chicken stock
	pepper	1	cup heavy cream
1	Tbls. minced garlic	1	cup whole milk
¼	tsp. nutmeg	1	pint oysters

Boil the artichokes for about 30 to 45 minutes until leaves pull off easily. Scrape the leaves and clean and chop the bottoms. If using canned hearts, drain, rinse them well and coarsely chop. Set aside.

In a large heavy bottomed Dutch oven, melt the butter and add the celery onion and bell pepper. Sauté over a medium heat until the vegetables are soft but not browned. Stir in the garlic, nutmeg, sage, thyme, black, white and cayenne peppers and salt. Cook for 1 minute. Add the flour, mixing well to avoid any lumps. Cook and stir for 1 minute. Blend in the chicken stock , add the artichoke scrapings and bottoms (or hearts), and bring to a gentle boil. Cover and simmer for 10 minutes. Add the cream and milk and return to a simmer, stirring occasionally. Pour in the oysters and a little of the oyster liquor and cook just until their edges are curled, about 5 minutes. Adjust the seasoning and serve.

OYSTER STEW

Serves 6

In 1937 President Roosevelt traveled to New Orleans to dedicate the Roosevelt Mall in City Park. During a banquet in his honor, which included oysters, our illustious Mayor Maestri reportedly leaned toward the president and eloquently enquired "How you like dem ersters?" Whatever you call them, this simple and elegant dish is a great way to enjoy the delicate flavor of freshly shucked oysters.

½ cup butter
¼ cup thinly sliced green onions
½ tsp. white pepper
1 pinch cayenne pepper
1 cup heavy cream
3 cups whole milk
2 tsp. salt (or to taste)
3 pints freshly shucked oysters

Melt the butter over a medium heat in a large non-reactive saucepan. Add the green onions and sauté for a minute or two until they begin to soften. Stir in the white pepper and cayenne pepper, then add the cream, milk and salt.

Separate the oysters from their liquor and strain the liquor into the pot. Bring the mixture to a simmer. Cook for 3 minutes, stirring often. Add the oysters and simmer another 3 to 5 minutes, or until the edges curl.

Adjust the seasoning and serve immediately.

CREOLE GAZPACHO
Serves 10 to 12

2	lbs. cucumbers, peeled and seeded	46	ounces vegetable juice (such as V-8)
3-4	large ripe Creole tomatoes, about 3 lbs. total	1	Tbls. minced garlic
2½	cups chopped yellow bell peppers, about ¼-inch dice	1¼	cups extra virgin olive oil
		½	cup red wine vinegar
2½	cups chopped green bell peppers, about ¼-inch dice	½	cup chopped fresh basil
		1	Tbls. salt (or to taste)
2½	cups chopped onion, about ¼-inch dice	1	Tbls. white pepper
		1	tsp. Tabasco sauce (or to taste)

Have all ingredients chilled. Chop the cucumbers to about a ¼-inch dice. Core the tomatoes and chop into ½-inch pieces. Combine the cucumbers and tomatoes with the remaining ingredients in a large crockery bowl or stainless steel container and mix well. Remove about a quart of the mixture to a blender or food processor and puree, then stir it back into the soup. Chill at least 8 hours before serving to allow the flavors to marry. Serve in chilled bowls and, if desired, garnish with a dollop of sour cream, or as some of our customers request, a shot of vodka.

This recipe makes a lot — about 5 quarts, and will stay fresh in the refrigerator for only three or four days — but on hot summer days it is so tasty, light and refreshing it is hard to stop eating it.

Although this dish is not considered an old local tradition, we think it should be. All the essential elements are there — the early Spanish influence, luscious vine ripened Creole tomatoes, locally grown peppers and beastly hot summer days. We introduced this soup about ten years ago at the restaurant, and it has been a hit every summer since.

CORN AND CRAWFISH CHOWDER

Serves 8 to 10

¼	lb. sliced bacon, cut into 1-inch pieces	¼	cup finely chopped tasso
1	cup chopped onions	½	lb. coarsely chopped carrots
¾	cup chopped green bell pepper	½	lb. peeled red potatoes, cut into ¼-inch dice
1	Tbls. minced garlic	1	lb. fresh or frozen corn kernels
½	tsp. black pepper	2	15 ounce can creamed corn
1	tsp. white pepper	3	cups chicken stock
½	tsp. cayenne pepper	1	cup heavy cream
2	bay leaves	1	lb. peeled crawfish tails
½	tsp. thyme	½	cup finely chopped green onions
1½	tsp. salt		

Set a large heavy bottomed Dutch oven over medium heat, add the bacon and cook, stirring occasionally, until the bacon pieces are crisp. Remove the bacon with a slotted spoon and set aside. Add the onion and bell pepper to the rendered bacon fat and sauté, stirring occasionally, until tender. Add the garlic and cook for 1 minute. Add the black, white and cayenne pepper, the bay leaves, thyme and salt. Stir in the bacon and the tasso and cook for 1 minute. Add the carrots, potatoes and corn kernels. Mix well and cook for 2 to 3 minutes.

Add the creamed corn and cook for 1 minute, stirring well. Slowly stir in the chicken stock and bring to a slow boil. Cover and simmer for about 15 minutes or until carrots and potatoes are tender. Blend in the cream and add the crawfish. Return to a gentle simmer, adjust the seasoning and cook for 5 minutes.

Serve in large soup plates, garnishing each with a tablespoon of chopped green onion.

TURTLE SOUP

Serves 8 to 10

2	lbs. boneless turtle meat	½	tsp. thyme
2	lbs. turtle bones or beef bones	½	tsp. nutmeg
¾	cup butter	½	tsp. grated lemon zest
½	cup flour	¼	tsp. cayenne pepper
2	cups minced onion	1	tsp. black pepper
1¼	cups minced green bell pepper	3	tsp. salt
1¼	cups minced celery	4	cups chopped tomatoes, fresh or canned
1	Tbls. minced garlic	5	cups turtle stock
½	tsp. rosemary	1	Tbls. Worcestershire sauce
¼	tsp. ground cloves	1	Tbls. lemon juice
4	bay leaves	⅓	cup dry sherry
½	tsp. basil	2	hard boiled eggs, chopped
½	tsp. ground allspice		

Place the turtle (or beef) bones in a stock pot and cover with water. Bring the pot to a boil, lower the heat and simmer for at least 4 hours. Remove the bones from the pot and add the turtle meat. Simmer until tender, about 1 hour. Remove and set aside.

In a large heavy bottomed Dutch oven melt the butter over a medium high heat and whisk in the flour. Make a dark brown roux. (See roux photo, page 10) When the proper color has been attained add the minced onion, bell pepper and celery and cook until tender. Allow the vegetables to stick to the bottom of the pot from time to time, scraping them up with a metal spoon. Add the garlic and spices. Cook for 1 minute. Add the chopped tomatoes and cook for about 15 minutes, repeating the sticking and scraping process.

Stir in 5 cups of the turtle (or beef) stock and the Worcestershire sauce. Bring the pot to a boil. Reduce the heat, partially cover the pot and simmer for 30 minutes, stirring occasionally.

Meanwhile, chop the cooked and cooled turtle meat into about a ½-inch dice. Add it to the pot along with the lemon juice and sherry. Bring the pot to a boil, lower the heat and simmer for 20 to 30 minutes. Adjust the seasoning and add a little more stock if the soup is too thick. Serve in large soup plates garnished with chopped hard boiled eggs and more sherry if desired.

SALADS
AND DRESSINGS

The New Orleans area's climate and soil are kind to vegetables. Creole tomatoes, for example, a robust and flavorful crop, are nurtured by the soil of the Mississippi delta and incubated in the semitropical climate.

Among the salad dressing recipes you will find in this chapter is one for "remoulade." Of French origin, the primary ingredients are mayonnaise and Creole mustard with assorted seasonings. Culinary historian John Mariani notes that the word is derived from "ramolas," meaning horseradish. The word comes from the northern French dialect of the Picardy Region. In New Orleans there's more of a kick to the taste than the traditional French version.

— PSL

WILD PECAN RICE
AND RED BEAN SALAD

Serves 8

For those Mondays when it is just too hot to eat the traditional Red Beans and Rice. Wild pecan rice is a brown rice with a nutty flavor that smells like popcorn when it is cooking. A strain of Basmati rice, it is farmed in Crowley, Louisiana.

1	cup wild pecan rice	1	Tbls. chopped parsley
¼	tsp. salt	1	Tbls. chopped fresh basil
2	cups water	¼	tsp. cayenne pepper
¾	cup roasted pecan halves	¼	tsp. white pepper
1	15 ounce can red kidney beans, drained and rinsed	¼	tsp. black pepper
½	cup chopped green onions	½	tsp. salt
½	cup chopped red bell pepper	½	cup Vinaigrette Dressing, page 40

Combine the water and salt in a 1 or 2 quart pot with a tight fitting lid. Bring to a boil and add the rice. Stir, return to a boil, lower the heat, cover and simmer for 25 minutes or until rice is tender and all water is absorbed. Transfer the rice to a large bowl and fluff it up to allow the heat to escape. When the rice is cool, combine the remaining ingredients and mix with the rice.

CREOLE TOMATOES VINAIGRETTE

Serves 4

4 ripe Creole tomatoes, about
   ½ lb. each
4 cups spring mix or torn
   lettuce leaves (such as
   Boston or Bibb)

½ cup vinaigrette dressing
   About 8 large fresh basil
   leaves

Line four chilled plates with the spring mix or lettuce. Core the tomatoes and cut each one into 4 thick crosswise slices. Tear each basil leaf into several pieces. Arrange the tomato slices over the lettuce, drizzle each with 2 tablespoons of vinaigrette and sprinkle with basil.

VINAIGRETTE DRESSING

Makes about 2 cups

½ cup Balsamic vinegar
1 tsp. salt
½ tsp. black pepper

2 tsp. dry mustard
1 tsp. minced garlic
1½ cups extra virgin olive oil

Combine the first 5 ingredients in a non reactive bowl and mix well with a wire whip. Slowly drizzle in the olive oil while beating constantly.

Simple, elegant and satisfying, it is the quality of the ingredients that count.

Creole tomatoes are not really a variety, but a vine ripened tomato grown in the alluvial soil of southeast Louisiana, ripening during the early summer. Big, meaty and kind of ugly, the Creole tomato is produced by a combination of soil, heat and moisture, and is not a variety. Although some people at LSU once developed a seed they called Creole, local growers use several varieties including Big Boy, Better Boy and Beefstake. When outside of New Orleans, use only the best locally grown, vine ripened tomatoes you can get your hands on.

BLACKENED CHICKEN SALAD
Serves 4

½ tsp. black pepper
½ tsp. white pepper
½ tsp. cayenne pepper
½ tsp. thyme
½ tsp. basil
½ tsp. granulated garlic
½ tsp. onion powder
1 tsp. salt

2 boneless, skinless chicken
   breasts, about 8 ounces each
2 Tbls. butter, melted
1 cup New Orleans Italian
   Dressing, page 42
8 cups spring mix or torn
   lettuce leaves
2 large vine ripened tomatoes,
   cut in wedges

Combine seasoning and mix well. Dredge the chicken breast in the butter
and sprinkle both sides with the spice mixture. Heat a 10 or 12 inch black iron
skillet over a very high heat for 5 minutes. Carefully place the chicken breast in
the pan. Cook for 2 minutes, turn and cook the other side for 1 to 2 minutes
until done. (Blackening creates a lot of smoke — be sure you have adequate
ventilation. Also, have a large pot lid or pizza pan handy to cover the pan in
case the butter in the pan catches on fire.)

Allow the blackened chicken breast to cool a bit and slice into strips about
½-inch thick. In a small bowl, toss the chicken with the New Orleans Italian
Dressing. Divide the greens between four large plates. Top each with chicken
and garnish with tomato wedges.

New Orleans Italian Dressing

Makes 1¾ cups

Hailing mainly from Sicily, the influx of Italians to the New Orleans area occured around the turn of the century. Their influence on the local cuisine is often underestimated or unmentioned. Considering the climate, culture and pantry of Sicily, these new Americans slipped into New Orleans like a hand into a glove. At one time the French Quarter was considered an Italian neighborhood. Central Grocery on Decatur Street dress their famous Muffeletta sandwiches with an olive salad that was the inspiration for this salad dressing.

¼	tsp. cayenne pepper	1	Tbls. minced anchovies or anchovy paste
¼	tsp. white pepper		
¼	tsp. black pepper	2	Tbls. chopped pimentos
½	tsp. sugar	1	Tbls. drained capers
½	tsp. oregano	2	Tbls. sliced black olives
½	tsp. salt	3	Tbls. chopped green olives
½	tsp. dry mustard	⅓	cup Balsamic vinegar
1	Tbls. chopped green onions	1	cup extra virgin olive oil
1	tsp. minced garlic		

Combine the peppers, sugar, oregano salt and dry mustard, then mix well with the remaining ingredients.

REMOULADE SAUCE

Makes 2 cups

½ cup plus 2 Tbls. Creole
    mustard (see glossary,
    page 111)
½ cup mayonnaise, preferably
    Homemade Mayonnaise,
    page 46
⅓ cup cooking oil
1 Tbls. olive oil
3 Tbls. minced celery

3 Tbls. minced green onion
1 tsp. minced garlic
1 Tbls. lemon juice
1 Tbls. Worcestershire sauce
1 tsp. Tabasco sauce
2 Tbls. paprika
1 tsp. white pepper
½ tsp. cayenne pepper
1 tsp. salt

Combine all ingredients in a stainless steel, glass or crockery bowl. Cover and refrigerate for 4 hours or overnight before serving. This recipe makes about 2 cups, or enough for 1 pound of boiled peeled shrimp or crawfish tails.

To serve mix the shrimp or crawfish with the sauce and divide among six or eight chilled plates that have been lined with chopped lettuce. Garnish with lemon wedges.

This sauce is also wonderful as a dip for raw or lightly steamed vegetables.

There are two primary renditions of remoulade sauce available in most New Orleans restaurants — a reddish one and a whitish one, both very different from the classic French version. We call the reddish one "remoulade sauce" and the whitish one "white remoulade sauce." At the Gumbo Shop we further fog one's understanding, as our house salad dressing, which we sometimes call "Creole French dressing" is the same as a white remoulade sauce. In fact, we served this dressing for years before its popularization as white remoulade. The following recipe is for the reddish one, which we serve with shrimp and/or crawfish.

WHITE REMOULADE SAUCE (HOUSE DRESSING)

Makes 2 cups

½ cup Creole mustard (see glossary, page 111)
1 cup mayonnaise, preferably Homemade
    Mayonnaise, page 46
¼ cup finely chopped green bell pepper
¼ cup finely chopped celery

Combine ingredients, mix well, cover and refrigerate for 4 hours or overnight before using.

Use this as you would the other remoulade sauce, or serve small portions of both on the same plate.

FISH SAUCE

Makes 2 cups

1 cup Creole mustard (see glossary, page 111)
1 16 ounce jar sweet orange marmalade
1 Tbls. catsup
1 Tbls. prepared horseradish

Combine all the ingredients and mix well. Refrigerate covered for about 4 hours or overnight before serving. Use as a dipping sauce for grilled or blackened fish and chicken.

For lack of a better name "Fish Sauce" is what we call the condiment we serve with most of our blackened or grilled items. Customers started asking for the recipe before we thought of a catchy and descriptive moniker.

HOMEMADE MAYONNAISE

Make 2 cups

1	Tbls. chopped shallot or onion
1	clove garlic, chopped
1	Tbls. fresh lemon juice
1	tsp. white wine vinegar
1	tsp. salt
1	pinch cayenne pepper
1	tsp. dry mustard
1	tsp. sugar
1	large egg
3	large egg yolks
1	cup chilled canola oil (or other mild vegetable oil)
¼	cup extra virgin olive oil

*M*ost locals grew up proclaiming this condiment "my-nez." While many still do, more and more simply say "mayo" — embarrassed by the family of origin vernacular but unwilling to suffer the shame of switching to the standard American pronunciation.

A good quality commercial mayonnaise will work well in most dishes, but homemade brings it up to another level. Besides, the ingredients are mostly kitchen staples, and a food processor makes the preparation quick and easy. This recipe yields a rich and flavorful spread. Vary the amount of salt, pepper and lemon juice to taste.

In the bowl of a food processor fitted with the metal cutting blade, combine the onion or shallot, garlic, lemon juice, vinegar, salt, pepper, mustard, sugar, egg and egg yolks. Process about 1 minute until the onion and garlic are pureed and the salt and sugar are dissolved.

With the motor running, slowly pour in the canola oil in a pencil lead thin stream. Add the olive oil in the same method. Turn the motor off and scrape the sides and top of the bowl, then process again for a few seconds. Adjust the seasoning and store in a covered container, refrigerated, for up to one week.

Mardi Gras Cole Slaw

Makes about 2 quarts

1½	lbs. thinly shredded green cabbage
½	lb. thinly shredded purple cabbage
¼	lb. grated carrot
1	cup mayonnaise, preferably Homemade Mayonnaise, page 46
½	cup Creole mustard (see glossary, page 111)
1	tsp. black pepper
1	tsp. white pepper
½	tsp. Tabasco sauce

A far cry from the bland, overly sweet variety offered on salad bars and in fast food restaurants. The symbolic Mardi Gras colors of purple (justice), green (faith) and gold (power) are reflected in the ingredients of this festive slaw.

To easily shred the cabbage, cut the head in quarters, cut out the core and slice each quarter as thinly as possible with a sharp chef knife or bread knife. Place the shredded cabbage in a colander and rinse under cold water, then spin dry in a salad spinner or spread on some toweling to remove excess moisture. Grate the carrot with a hand held grater and toss with the dry shredded cabbage.

Meanwhile, combine the mayonnaise, Creole mustard, black pepper, white pepper and Tabasco sauce and mix well.

Combine the dressing with the cabbage and carrots in a large non-reactive bowl and toss to mix. Cover and refrigerate for at least 4 hours before serving.

Note: Avoid using precut cole slaw mix as it is often dried out and lacking in flavor.

Roasted Pecan Vinaigrette

Makes about 2 cups

This variation on a vinaigrette has become one of our most popular salad dressings. The salad shown here is one of mixed field greens with Satsuma sections. Louisiana's citrus harvest gives us plentiful navel oranges, Satsumas and Kumquats.

⅓ cup minced onion
1 Tbls. minced garlic
¼ cup Balsamic vinegar
4 tsp. dry mustard
⅓ cup dark brown sugar
½ tsp. salt
½ tsp. black pepper
1 cup extra virgin olive oil
½ cup roasted pecan halves, coarsely chopped

Combine the first seven ingredients in a non reactive bowl and mix well with a wire whip. Slowly pour in the olive oil, beating constantly. Stir in the pecans. Serve over seasonal greens.

To roast pecan halves, spread them on a cookie sheet and place in a 350° oven. Roast for about 10 minutes until crisp and lightly browned, stirring every few minutes to prevent burning.

DONNA'S SPICY POTATO SALAD

Makes 2 quarts

Old fashioned potato salad with a twist — we boil small red new potatoes with crab boil and cayenne pepper for that signature New Orleans flavor.

2½	pounds small red new potatoes	1	cup celery, chopped
¼	cup salt	½	cup green onions, chopped
½	Tbls. cayenne pepper	¼	cup yellow mustard
1	3 ounce package dry crab boil	½	tsp. black pepper
¾	cups mayonnaise, preferably Homemade Mayonnaise, page 46	1	tsp. salt
		4	hard boiled eggs, peeled and chopped

Bring enough water to cover the potatoes to a boil in a stock pot with the salt, cayenne pepper, and dry crab boil. The longer the spice packet boils, the more intense the flavor. Add potatoes, cover and cook until potatoes are done, about 25 minutes. Drain the potatoes and allow to cool to room temperature.

Dice the potatoes, leaving the skin on. In a large bowl combine all the remaining ingredients and mix well. Add the potatoes and mix well again. Cover the salad and refrigerate for 4 hours before serving.

ENTRÉES

Of all the chapters in this cookbook, "Entrées" most reflects the city's diverse ethnic influences. One dish alone, Jambalaya, has roots that combine French, Spanish and West African influences. In Louisiana, a bit of Cajun spice has been added to the dish as well. All these influences, plus a touch of German, are, quite literally, mixed in the pot at the "Jambalaya Festival" in Gonzales, Louisiana, 30 miles up the Mississippi River from New Orleans. The inclusion of alligator and tasso, a spicy smoked pork, as ingredients for some of the following recipes underscores the variety of influences.

Contemporary Cajun cooking has introduced "blackening," a technique that involves nearly charring, in a skillet, the exterior of fish or poultry in a coat of seasoning while locking in the flavors. In great Louisiana dishes, the tastes are as varied as the influences that created them.

— PSL

JAMBALAYA

Serves 6 to 8

1	lb. chicken breasts and thighs, bone in	1	16 ounce can crushed tomatoes
	about 3 cups water to cover	½	tsp. white pepper
¼	cup cooking oil	½	tsp. black pepper
½	lb. smoked sausage, sliced into ¼-inch rounds	¼	tsp. cayenne pepper
		1	tsp. salt
2	cups chopped onion	1	cup converted long grain rice
½	cup chopped green bell pepper	1½	cups stock (from cooking chicken)
½	cup chopped celery	1	lb. peeled shrimp
2	tsp. minced garlic		

Cover the chicken with water and set over a medium heat. Bring to a boil, reduce the heat and simmer for about 45 minutes. Remove the chicken from the pot and reserve the stock. When cool enough to handle, remove the chicken meat from the bones and skin and cut it into bite sized pieces. Set aside. Reserve stock.

Meanwhile, in a large heavy bottomed Dutch oven over a medium heat, sauté the sausage in the oil until lightly browned. Remove it from the pot with a slotted spoon and set it aside with the chicken. Add the onion, celery and bell pepper to the pot and sauté until tender. Add the crushed tomatoes, garlic, salt and pepper and cook for about 10 minutes, stirring and scraping the bottom of the pot. Stir in the rice and mix well. Stir in 1½ cups of the reserved chicken stock, bring the pot to a boil and then reduce to a simmer. Add the sausage, chicken and raw peeled shrimp. Cook uncovered, stirring occasionally, until the rice and shrimp are done, about 20 minutes.

Illustrating the passion with which locals embrace their food and culture, during a recent two week period there appeared four letters to the editor of the Times Picayune "proving" that the origin of Jambalaya was Spanish, then French, then West African, then Spanish again. The Spanish word for ham (a common Jambalaya ingredient) is "jamon," and the dish has it's similarities with the Spanish dish paella. The French Provençal term "jambalaia" translates as "a stew made of rice and fowl." The West African word "jambe" means "to mix" or "a melange". Whatever the linguistic or culinary origin, and there is likely truth in all these explanations, Jambalaya is easy to prepare and makes a delicious one dish meal.

SHRIMP CREOLE

Serves 6

A staple of New Orleans home kitchens, especially during the early summer months when fresh shrimp are plentiful and vine ripened local tomatoes are at their best. This is the essential Creole Sauce — keep the method of preparation and the seasonings the same and let your imagination fly. Use any kind of stock you wish, substitute fish, fowl, or vegetables for the shrimp, and serve over omelettes, pasta or grains instead of the usual rice. In these pages we include several recipes which utilize this versatile sauce.

3	lbs. head on shrimp, about 30-40 count per lb.
	water to cover
½	cup butter
¼	cup flour
1	cup finely chopped onion
½	cup finely chopped celery
½	cup finely chopped green bell pepper
1	tsp. sugar
½	tsp. white pepper
½	tsp. black pepper
¼	tsp. cayenne pepper
2	whole bay leaves
½	tsp. thyme
½	tsp. salt
½	tsp. basil
½	tsp. Tabasco sauce
1	cup chopped tomatoes, fresh or canned
1	cup tomato sauce
1	Tbls. olive oil
½	cup onion, sliced into ¼-inch strips
½	cup celery, cut across the stalk at a 45 degree angle into ¼-inch strips
½	cup green bell pepper, sliced into ¼-inch strips

Peel and devein the shrimp, cover and set aside in the refrigerator. Rinse the heads and shells, place them in a saucepan with just enough water to cover and bring to a boil over a medium heat. Reduce to a simmer and cook for 30 to 45 minutes to make a stock. Strain and set aside.

Meanwhile melt the butter in a large heavy bottomed non reactive Dutch oven set over a medium heat. Stir in the flour and make a medium brown peanut butter colored roux. (See roux photo, page 10) Immediately add the finely chopped onion, celery and bell pepper, stirring well to mix. Cook until the vegetables are soft and start to brown, stirring and scraping the bottom of the pot often. Add the sugar and spices, the Tabasco, the chopped tomatoes and tomato sauce and cook for 15 minutes, stirring and scraping the bottom often. Stir in one cup of shrimp stock and return to a slow boil. Simmer for about 5 minutes.

While the sauce is simmering heat the olive oil over a high heat in a large skillet. Add the sliced onion, celery and bell pepper and stir fry for about 3 minutes. Add it to the sauce along with the peeled shrimp. Return to a gentle boil and simmer for 8 to 10 minutes, being careful not to overcook the shrimp. Serve over steamed rice.

CRAWFISH AND PASTA IN TASSO CREAM
Serves 4

½ lb. good quality dried pasta, either Penne or Rotini	2 cups heavy cream
4 Tbls. butter	1 tsp. white pepper
¼ lb. tasso, finely chopped	½ tsp. cayenne pepper
1 cup thinly sliced green onions	1 tsp. salt (or to taste)
2 tsp. minced garlic	½ lb. peeled crawfish tails

Cook the pasta according to the package directions, being careful not to overcook. Rinse in cold water and set aside.

Melt the butter in a large skillet. Add the tasso and sauté until lightly browned. Add the garlic and green onions. Cook, stirring for one minute. Add the cream, white pepper, cayenne pepper and salt while stirring constantly, bring to a boil and cook for about two minutes until slightly thickened. Add the crawfish tails, return to a boil and cook for one minute. Add the pasta, mix in well, and cook until the pasta is heated through. Serve immediately in warmed plates or bowls.

Tasso, sometimes referred to as Cajun bacon or ham is heavily smoked and peppered dried pork used as seasoning in a myriad of dishes. It works particularly well in cream based sauces such as this one.

SHRIMP AND PASTA WITH SMOKED TOMATO MARINARA

Serves 6

2 lbs. diced tomatoes, fresh
   or canned, divided
⅓ cup extra virgin olive oil
⅔ cup chopped onions
¼ lb. small mushrooms,
   quartered
1 Tbls. minced garlic
2 tsp. salt

1 tsp. black pepper
1 tsp. dried oregano
1 Tbls. chopped fresh basil
1 lb. peeled shrimp, medium
   size
¾ lb. dried pasta, such as penne
   or rotini

Spread 1 pound of the diced tomatoes on a small roasting pan and smoke for 20 minutes in a backyard smoker or covered barbecue grill according to the manufacturer's directions. Set aside.

In a large saucepan set over a medium heat, sauté the chopped onion in the olive oil until tender. Add the mushrooms, garlic, salt, pepper and oregano and cook for 1 minute. Add the smoked tomatoes, the other pound of diced tomatoes and bring the pot to a boil. Reduce the heat and simmer for 5 minutes. Add the shrimp and cook for about 5 minutes, until the shrimp are just done. Stir in the basil and turn off the heat.

Meanwhile, cook the pasta according to the package directions. Drain well and toss with the sauce in a large preheated bowl. Serve immediately.

CRAWFISH ETOUFFEE

Serves 4

Simple and quick to prepare, especially now with the availability of peeled crawfish tails. Be sure to use fresh ones that have not been frozen or rinsed. If not available from your local fish market, try one of the mail order sources listed in the back of this book.

½ cup butter
¼ cup flour
3 cups chopped onion
½ cup chopped celery
½ cup chopped green bell pepper
2 tsp. minced garlic
½ tsp. basil
½ tsp. black pepper
½ tsp. white pepper

¼ tsp. cayenne pepper
1 tsp. salt (or to taste)
1 tsp. paprika
½ tsp. Tabasco sauce
1¼ cup shrimp stock or chicken stock
1 lb. peeled crawfish tails
½ cup thinly sliced green onions
1 Tbls. chopped parsley

Set a large heavy bottomed Dutch oven over a medium heat. Melt the butter, add the flour and make a roux the color of peanut butter. (See roux photo, page 10). Add the chopped onion, celery and bell pepper. Cook until the onions are translucent and the celery and bell pepper are tender. Add the garlic, basil, black pepper, white pepper, cayenne pepper, salt and paprika and cook for two minutes. Stir in the Tabasco sauce and stock and bring to a gentle boil. Add the crawfish tails, green onions and parsley. Simmer for about 5 minutes, stirring occasionally. Serve over steamed rice.

REDFISH CREOLE

Serves 4

4   redfish fillets, about
      6-8 ounces each
1   Tbls. melted butter
2   tsp. Seasoning Mix, page 73
2   cups Shrimp Creole, page 56

Here's a way to use leftovers from Shrimp Creole. With the proliferation of fish farming operations around the country, redfish are now available at many fish markets. If not, just about any firm, flaky mild tasting white fleshed fish will do.

Preheat a gas or charcoal grill according to the manufacturer's directions. Brush the fish fillets with the melted butter and sprinkle with seasoning mix. Grill the fillets for about two minutes on one side, turn and cook one minute on the other side or until just done. Meanwhile, heat the Shrimp Creole in a small saucepan. When the fish is done, remove to four warm plates and spoon about ½ cup of sauce over each fillet. Serve immediately.

TROUT FLORENTINE

Serves 4

This is a very "restaurant style" dish. It is cooked to order, meant to be served immediately, and requires several prepared items to be warm and on hand.

4	Speckled trout fillets, about 6 ounces each	2	cups Creole Creamed Spinach, page 86
2	Tbls. melted butter	1	cup Hollandaise Sauce, following
2	tsp. Seasoning Mix, page 73		

Have the creamed spinach and hollandaise sauce set aside, at serving temperature. Dredge the trout fillets in the butter, sprinkle with the seasoning mix, and either grill, broil or bake until just done.

On four warmed plates, spread a bed of ½ cup of creamed spinach. Place a cooked trout fillet on top of each one, then top each fillet with ¼ cup of Hollandaise Sauce. Serve immediately.

HOLLANDAISE SAUCE

Makes 2½ cups

6	large egg yolks	1	dash Tabasco sauce
1	Tbls. plus 1 tsp. fresh lemon juice	¼	tsp. white pepper
		1	lb. butter, melted and still hot

Combine the egg yolks, lemon juice, Tabasco sauce and white pepper in the canister of an electric blender. Blend at high speed for a few seconds to mix. Remove the center of the lid and, with the motor running, slowly drizzle in the melted butter. Turn the motor off, scrape down the sides of the canister with a rubber spatula, and blend a few seconds more.

This may be prepared up to an hour before use and kept warm in a wide mouth insulated thermal container.

ALLIGATOR SAUCE PIQUANTE

Serves 8

1½	lbs. alligator tail meat	1	Tbls. minced fresh jalapeño
	Butter for sautéing		peppers
½	cup butter	1	Tbls. minced garlic
¼	cup flour	¼	tsp. Tabasco sauce
½	cup finely chopped onion	½	tsp. white pepper
⅓	cup finely chopped celery	¼	tsp. black pepper
⅓	cup finely chopped green bell	¼	tsp. cayenne pepper
	pepper	1½	tsp. salt
1	cup chopped onion	1	cup crushed tomatoes
⅔	cup chopped celery	2	cups diced tomatoes, fresh
⅔	cup chopped green bell		or canned
	pepper	3	cups chicken stock

Slice the alligator meat across the grain into slices about ¼-inch or a bit thicker, then cut any large slices into bite sized pieces. In a large, heavy bottomed Dutch oven, melt some butter and sauté the alligator pieces over a medium heat until lightly browned. Remove the meat from the pot, drain and set aside.

Measure the butter left in the pot and add more, if necessary, to equal ½ cup. Return the butter to the same pot, set it over a medium heat and stir in the flour. Cook and stir to make a medium roux, the color of peanut butter. (See roux photo, page 10) Add the finely chopped onion, celery and bell pepper. Cook, stirring and scraping the bottom often for about 5 minutes until tender and lightly browned. Add the chopped onion, celery and bell pepper, the minced jalapeño and garlic and cook until tender, about 8 minutes. Stir in the Tabasco sauce, white pepper, black pepper, cayenne pepper and salt.

Once on the brink of extinction, alligators have made such a strong comeback in Louisiana's swamps and bayous that hunting this ancient reptilian specie is now encouraged. A cross shaped bone runs the length of an alligator's tail, dividing the flesh into four long tapering "tenderloins" of white meat. The body meat is dark, tough and sinewy, and should be avoided. The mild flavor of alligator makes a fine vehicle for this spicy sauce.

(continued on page 67)

Add the crushed tomatoes and diced tomatoes. Cook for 10 minutes, stirring and scraping the bottom of the pot from time to time. Add the chicken stock, bring to a boil, reduce the heat and simmer for 10 minutes. Add the sautéed alligator meat, return to a boil and simmer for 20 minutes, or until alligator is tender. Adjust the seasoning and serve over steamed rice.

CHICKEN SAUCE PIQUANTE

Equally as delicious as its more exotic counterpart, simply substitute 1½ pounds of cooked boneless chicken meat for the alligator. The chicken may be roasted, grilled or sautéed as described above.

GRILLADES AND GRITS

Serves 6

Many New Orleanians were raised on grillades, served with grits for a hearty breakfast or brunch, or over rice for a casual dinner.

1 lb. veal round	¼ cup chopped green onions
Salt and white pepper for seasoning	1 Tbls. minced garlic
Flour for dredging	2 cups chopped tomatoes, fresh or canned
⅔ cup butter, or more if necessary	1 cup beef stock
⅓ cup flour	¾ cup red wine
⅔ cup chopped onion	½ tsp. Tabasco sauce
1 cup chopped bell pepper	1 Tbls. Worcestershire sauce
½ cup chopped celery	4 cups cooked yellow grits

Cut the meat into pieces about 1-inch by 2-inch, season with salt and white pepper and dredge in flour to coat. In a large black iron pan set over a medium high heat, melt the butter and sauté the meat until browned on each side. Remove from the pan and set aside.

Measure the butter left in the pan and adjust to equal ½ cup. Return the butter to the pan and stir well, scraping up any bits of meat or flour that may be stuck to the bottom. Set the pan over a medium heat, stir in the flour and make a dark brown roux. (See roux photo, page 10) Add the chopped onion, green bell pepper and celery and cook until tender and the onions are slightly browned. Add the green onions and garlic and cook for one minute. Stir in the tomatoes and cook for about 15 minutes, stirring occasionally and scraping the bottom of the pan. Add stock, wine, Tabasco and Worcestershire. Bring to a boil, add the sautéed meat and simmer until tender.

Adjust the seasoning and serve over grits.

CHICKEN ESPAGNOLE

Serves 6

3 small chickens,
    about 2 lbs. each
    Seasoning Mix, page 73
1 lb. chicken wings, backs or
    other parts for making
    stock
¾ cup butter
¾ cup flour
2 cups finely chopped onion
¾ cup finely chopped celery

¾ cup finely chopped green bell
    pepper
1 tsp. minced garlic
½ tsp. rubbed sage
1 tsp. thyme
1 tsp. black pepper
1 tsp. white pepper
2 tsp. salt
1 lb. mushrooms, sliced
½ cup thinly sliced green onions
½ cup chopped parsley

A Gumbo Shop standard, this dish appeared on the menu at a time and of an origin that no one remembers. Major misnomer notwithstanding, it has remained popular through the years, probably because of its down home comfort food qualities. Classically speaking, "Espagnole" denotes a brown sauce made with beef stock. Our sauce for this dish is brown in color, but based on a concentrated roasted chicken stock, and spiced up a bit.

Cut each chicken in half, removing the backbone. Set chicken halves aside. Arrange the chicken backs and the 1 pound of chicken pieces for stock on a roasting pan sheet. Place in a preheated 400° oven and roast for 25 minutes or until the skin is brown. Place in a stock pot, cover with 2 quarts of water and set over a high heat. Bring to a boil, reduce the heat and simmer for about two hours.

Arrange the chicken halves on a roasting pan, sprinkle generously with the seasoning mix and roast in a preheated 400° oven for about 35 minutes or until the skin is browned. Remove from the oven and set aside.

Meanwhile, in a large heavy bottomed Dutch oven melt the butter over a medium heat, stir in the flour and make a dark brown roux. (See roux chart, page 10) As soon as the proper color is attained, add the onion, celery and bell pepper. Cook for about 20 minutes, stirring and scraping the bottom of the pot from time to time, until the vegetables are tender. Add the garlic, sage, thyme,

(continued on page 71)

white pepper, black pepper and salt and cook for one minute. Slowly stir in 4 cups of the stock, bring to a boil, reduce the heat and simmer for 20 minutes, stirring occasionally. Add the mushrooms, green onions and parsley and cook for one minute. Remove the pot from the heat.

Pour the sauce over the chicken halves in the roasting pan and return the pan to the oven, reducing the heat to 350°. Roast for about 20 minutes or until chicken is thoroughly done. Serve with steamed rice, spooning lots of sauce over the rice and the chicken halves.

BLACKENED OR GRILLED CHICKEN
Serves 4

A *New Orleans touch added to the ubiquitous boneless chicken breast.*

4 boneless, skinless chicken breasts, 6-8 ounces each
¼ cup Balsamic vinegar
¼ tsp. salt
¼ tsp. black pepper
1 tsp. dry mustard

½ tsp. minced garlic
¾ cup extra virgin olive oil
2 tsp. Seasoning Mix, or to taste, page 73
4 Tbls. melted butter

Rinse the chicken breasts and trim off any fat or skin. Combine the vinegar, salt, pepper, mustard and garlic in a small bowl and mix well with a wire whip. Slowly drizzle in the olive oil while beating constantly. Place the chicken breasts in a non-reactive bowl or baking dish and cover with the marinade. Cover and refrigerate at least eight hours, turning once or twice.

To cook, set a heavy black iron skillet over a medium high heat for five minutes. Meanwhile remove the breasts from the marinade, dredge in the melted butter and sprinkle with the seasoning mix. Carefully place the breasts in the hot pan. Do not crowd them and make sure you have plenty of ventilation as this process creates a lot of smoke. Cook for two minutes, turn and cook 2 minutes or until done. Serve right away, with a little mustard marmalade sauce (Fish Sauce, page 45) on the side.

SEASONING MIX

1 tsp. oregano
2 tsp. thyme
2 tsp. cayenne pepper
4 tsp. black pepper
4 tsp. white pepper
5 tsp. onion powder
5 tsp. garlic powder
2 Tbls. paprika
6 Tbls. salt

Combine and mix well. Store in a tightly sealed container.

This makes about ¾ cup and can be used for any grilled or roasted meat, fish or poultry.

Every good cook knows that really delicious food depends on fresh ingredients. The herbs and spices used in good cooking must be fresh, too. Buy these in small amounts and periodically go through the pantry tossing out herbs and spices that are too old.

BEANS, GREENS AND VEGETABLES

In Louisiana we grow fresh vegetables throughout the year. In the summer, dots of red, purple and green color gardens as tomatoes, eggplants, bell peppers, okra, corn and beans reach the picking stage. The cooler months yield a harvest of cabbage, potatoes, yams and mirlitons. With the emphasis on healthier cooking, the "stuff" your Mom urged you to eat has become fashionable.

Ironically, one of the city's signature dishes is made with a legume that isn't grown here at all. Red beans and rice is a native dish that is traditionally eaten on Mondays in New Orleans. The connection of the day to the dish may trace back to Monday being the day for washing clothes. With those chores to do, this was a dish that was little hassle. Slow cooking, one pot. Such a simple dish was a respite to the rich food consumed over the weekend. The hambone left over from Sunday dinner was thrown in the pot along with spices. After hours of cooking, the red beans become tender and ready to be ladled over rice.

— PSL

RED BEANS AND RICE

Serves 6

A tradition that has survived generations of culinary fashions and laundry routines.

1	lb. dry red kidney beans	¼	cup finely chopped celery
2	quarts water	2	tsp. minced garlic
1	ham bone, about ½ lb.	½	tsp. thyme
1	bay leaf	½	tsp. sage
¼	cup rendered bacon fat or cooking oil	1	tsp. black pepper
		1	tsp. white pepper
1½	cup finely chopped onion	¼	tsp. cayenne pepper
½	cup finely chopped green bell pepper	2	tsp. salt (or to taste)

Rinse the beans well and sort through them, removing any small rocks or other foreign objects. Place them in a large pot, cover with the water and soak in the refrigerator for at least eight hours.

Place the pot of beans over medium heat, add the ham bone and bay leaf and slowly bring to a boil, then reduce the heat to maintain a simmer. Meanwhile, set a large heavy skillet over a medium heat. Heat the rendered bacon fat or cooking oil and add the finely chopped onion, bell pepper and celery. Sauté until soft, then stir in the garlic, thyme, sage, black pepper, white pepper and cayenne pepper. Cook for 2 minutes and add to the simmering beans. Continue cooking until the beans are tender, adding more water if necessary. Add salt to taste. Remove about ¼ cup of cooked beans and mash them through a strainer, then mix them back into the pot. Simmer about ten more minutes and serve over steamed rice.

WHITE BEANS AND VEGETABLES

Serves 6

1 lb. dry Great Northern
   White Beans
2 quarts water
3 Tbls. olive oil
1 cup finely chopped onion
⅓ cup finely chopped shallots
1 tsp. minced fresh rosemary
½ tsp. black pepper
1 tsp. white pepper
¼ tsp. cayenne pepper
¼ cup dry vermouth
¼ cup olive oil
¼ cup minced garlic

½ lb. yellow squash, trimmed
   and sliced into ¼-inch
   rounds
½ lb. zucchini, trimmed and
   sliced into ¼-inch rounds
⅔ cup finely chopped red bell
   pepper
1 Tbls. salt
¼ tsp. Tabasco sauce
1 Tbls. Balsamic vinegar
1 Tbls. finely chopped fresh
   parsley

Through the years we have experienced increasing requests for vegetarian menu items. We developed several dishes, crafted around traditional techniques and ingredients, with lots of local flavor but no meat.

When fully cooked, white beans can easily turn into mush, so we use a double soaking method, allowing them to cook completely yet maintain their shape.

Rinse the beans well and sort through them, removing any small rocks or other foreign objects. Place them in a large pot, cover with the water and soak in the refrigerator for at least eight hours. Place the pot of beans over medium heat and slowly bring to a boil. Turn off the heat and let them soak at least one more hour at room temperature.

Over medium heat, return the pot to a boil then reduce the heat to maintain a slow simmer. Heat the olive oil in a large heavy skillet over medium heat. Add the onions and shallots and sauté until tender. Add the rosemary and cook for 2 minutes. Stir in the black pepper, white pepper and cayenne pepper and cook for one minute. Add the contents of the skillet to the pot of simmering beans and continue cooking until the beans are just tender, about 1 to 1½ hours.

Meanwhile, in the same skillet used to sauté the onions and shallots, heat the ¼ cup of olive oil. Add the minced garlic and sauté over a medium high heat until evenly browned. Add the yellow squash, zucchini and chopped red bell peppers, mix well and remove the pan from the heat. Set aside.

When the beans are done, add the browned garlic and vegetables, the vermouth, salt, Tabasco sauce and Balsamic vinegar. Bring the pot to a boil and cook for one minute. Stir in the parsley and remove the pot from the heat. Salt to taste. Serve over rice or pasta.

BLACK BEANS
WITH CREOLE TOMATO SALSA

Serves 6

T*hough not often found on New Orleans menus, black beans are among the tastiest of legumes and — considering the Caribbean and Hispanic influences on our local culture — deserve a place in the Creole pantry. One of our most popular vegetarian entrees, this spicy Cuban style dish is complemented with a cool fresh salsa.*

1	lb. black beans	1	tsp. white pepper
2	quarts water	1	tsp. black pepper
1	bay leaf	½	tsp. ground cumin
1	Tbls. olive oil	½	tsp. oregano
1¾	cups finely chopped onion	¼	cup olive oil
¾	cup finely chopped red bell pepper	¼	cup minced garlic
¾	cup finely chopped green bell pepper	2	tsp. Balsamic vinegar
1	Tbls. finely chopped jalapeño pepper (seeds removed)	½	tsp. Tabasco Sauce
		2	tsp. salt

Rinse the beans well and sort through them, removing any small rocks or other foreign objects. Place them in a large pot, cover with the water and soak in the refrigerator for at least eight hours.

Set the pot over medium heat and slowly bring to a boil, then reduce the heat to simmer. Add the bay leaf and cook until beans are tender, about 1 to 1½ hours, adding more water if necessary.

Meanwhile, in a large heavy skillet heat the olive oil over medium high heat and sauté the onions, bell peppers and jalapeños until tender. Stir in the white pepper, black pepper, cumin and oregano and cook for one minute. Add to the cooked black beans and simmer for about 15 minutes.

Heat the ¼ cup olive oil in a small sauce pan and add the minced garlic. Stir and cook until the garlic is evenly browned then immediately stir it into the beans. Add the Balsamic vinegar, then the Tabasco and salt to taste. Simmer for an additional 15 minutes. Serve over rice, garnished with about two tablespoons of Creole Tomato Salsa per serving.

CREOLE TOMATO SALSA

Makes 2 cups

1 lb. Creole or other vine
   ripened tomatoes, chopped

1 minced jalapeño pepper,
   seeds removed

1 Tbls. fresh lime juice
   Tabasco to taste

1 Tbls. fresh basil or parsley,
   chopped

½ tsp. salt

1 Tbls. olive oil

¼ cup diced green pepper

3 Tbls. minced shallot

Combine all the ingredients and refrigerate for at least one hour.

BLACK EYED PEAS AND RICE
Serves 6

These earthy tasting peas are popular all over the South, and New Orleans is no exception. Smothered Turnip Greens, page 84, and cornbread are the classic accompaniments.

1	lb. dried black eyed peas		¼	tsp. cayenne pepper
2	quarts water		½	tsp. sage
1	bay leaf		½	tsp. thyme
¼	cup olive oil		1½	cups celery, sliced into ½-inch slices
1¾	cup finely chopped onion			
1¼	cup finely chopped green bell pepper		½	lb. carrots, sliced into ½-inch thick rounds
¾	cup finely chopped shallot		1	tsp. salt
1	Tbls. minced garlic		½	tsp. Tabasco sauce
¼	tsp. white pepper		1½	tsp. Balsamic vinegar
¼	tsp. black pepper		⅓	cup sliced green onions

Rinse the peas well and sort through them, removing any small rocks or other foreign objects. Place them in a large pot, cover with the water and soak in the refrigerator for at least eight hours.

Set the pot over medium heat, add the bay leaf and slowly bring to a boil, then reduce the heat to maintain a simmer. Meanwhile, heat the olive oil in a large heavy skillet, add the chopped onions, peppers, garlic and shallots and sauté until lightly browned. Add the white pepper, black pepper, cayenne pepper, sage, thyme, celery and carrots and sauté for 5 minutes. Stir the entire contents of the skillet into the pot of simmering peas and continue cooking until the peas, celery and carrots are tender.

Add the salt, vinegar, Tabasco and green onions and simmer for an additional 10 minutes. Adjust the seasoning and serve over steamed rice.

SMOTHERED TURNIP GREENS

Serves 8

½ cup rendered bacon fat or olive oil
2 cups chopped onions
1 Tbls. minced garlic
¼ tsp. cayenne pepper
½ tsp. black pepper
2 tsp. salt
2 lbs. frozen chopped turnip greens, thawed
1 Tbls. white vinegar

Set a large sauce pan or a Dutch oven over a medium heat. Add the bacon fat or olive oil, chopped onions, garlic, cayenne pepper and black pepper. Sauté until the onions are soft. Add the salt and turnip greens, cover the pot and cook for 20 minutes, stirring occasionally. If necessary, lower the heat and add a little water to prevent scorching. Adjust the seasoning, add the vinegar and cook an additional 2 minutes.

SPICY BOILED NEW POTATOES
Serves 8

2½   lbs. small red new potatoes, cleaned
¼   cup salt
2   tsp. cayenne pepper
1   3-ounce package dry crab boil

Bring enough water to cover the potatoes to a boil in a stock pot with the salt, cayenne pepper and dry crab boil. The longer the spice packet boils the more intense the flavor. Add potatoes, cover and cook until the potatoes are done, about 25 minutes. Drain and serve.

In classical French cuisine a "bouquet garni" is often employed to enhance the flavor of stocks and broths. A few sprigs of thyme, a small bunch of parsley, some peppercorns, a bay leaf or two, and perhaps a few celery leaves are wrapped and bound in a small piece of cheesecloth then simmered in the liquid as a flavoring agent. Crab boil is like a bouquet garni gone buck wild. Encased in a small mesh pouch are 3 ounces of herbs and spices including mustard seed, coriander seed, cayenne pepper, bay leaves, dill seed, allspice and cloves — all to season just a few pounds of food. Of course you must also add some salt and additional pepper to spice it up a bit.

CREOLE CREAMED SPINACH

Serves 8

Seasoned with a lot of finely chopped onion and a hint of Herbsaint — the locally produced and legally available analogue of Absinthe. During the nineteenth century, Absinthe reigned as the drink of choice at many famous New Orleans watering holes. Extremely high in alcohol and infused with wormwood, it reputedly caused blindness or induced zombie-like states in the excessive enjoyer. After the sale of Absinthe was banned in the United States, Herbsaint was created to fill the flavor void without the nasty side effects. If Herbsaint is not available in your area Pernod will do. And for the daring and ambitious, it is rumored that several bars in Prague still serve real Absinthe.

2	lbs. chopped spinach, fresh or frozen	2	tsp. salt
2	cups water	¼	tsp. black pepper
2	Tbls. butter	¼	tsp. cayenne pepper
1½	cups finely chopped onion	½	tsp. white pepper
1	tsp. minced garlic	½	tsp. nutmeg
1	Tbls. flour	2	cups heavy cream
		2	tsp. Herbsaint or Pernod

In a large pot, bring the water to a boil, add the spinach, cover and cook for about 5 minutes. Remove from the heat and drain. Set aside. (If using frozen spinach, cook according to package directions and drain well.)

Melt the butter in a 4 quart stainless steel or enamelware pot. Add the finely chopped onions and sauté over a medium heat until tender. Add the garlic and spices. Cook for one minute. Stir in the flour, being careful not to let any lumps form. Cook and stir for 2 minutes. Stir in the heavy cream, bring to a simmer, and blend in the drained cooked spinach. Return to a simmer and cook for 10 minutes, stirring often. Add the Herbsaint or Pernod, cook one more minute and serve.

MACQUE CHOUX CORN

Serves 8

*P*ronounced *"mock shoe," this traditional Cajun dish made with sweet corn, seasonings and a little tomato is a tasty side dish for grilled or roasted chicken.*

1½ Tbls. butter
¼   cup chopped onion
⅓   cup chopped green bell pepper
½   tsp. minced garlic
½   tsp. sugar
½   tsp. white pepper
¼   tsp. black pepper
⅛   tsp. cayenne pepper
1   lb. yellow corn kernels, either frozen
    or cut from the cob
1   15 ounce can cream style corn
½   fresh ripe tomato, chopped, about ½ lb.
1   tsp. salt

Melt the butter over a medium heat in a large, heavy bottomed sauce pan. Add the chopped onion, bell pepper and garlic and sauté until tender. Add the white pepper, black pepper, cayenne pepper, sugar and corn kernels. Stir well, cover the pot and cook for about 15 minutes, stirring occasionally, until corn is tender. If necessary lower the heat and add a little water to prevent scorching. Add the cream style corn, chopped tomato and salt to taste. Bring the pot up to a simmer and cook for 5 more minutes.

STEWED OKRA AND TOMATOES

Serves 6

4 strips of bacon
1½ cups chopped onion
1 tsp. minced garlic
½ tsp. black pepper
½ tsp. white pepper
¼ tsp. cayenne pepper
1 lb. sliced okra, fresh or frozen
1 chopped tomato, fresh or canned
1 tsp. salt

In a large heavy bottomed skillet, fry the bacon over medium heat until crisp. Remove it from the pan and set aside. Add the chopped onion and the garlic to the pan and sauté in the bacon drippings until tender. Add the okra along with the three peppers and cook and stir until tender. Add the tomato and salt and simmer for 10 additional minutes. Crumble the cooked bacon into the pan, adjust the seasoning and serve.

THREE PO-BOYS

The quintessential New Orleans sandwich is the po-boy. In the 1920's two brothers named Benny and Clovis Martin, from the tiny Cajun community of Raceland, Louisiana, operated a sandwich stand in the French Market. In 1929, there was a tense strike of union streetcar operators. The Martins, having both been streetcar conductors, expressed their sympathy with the strikers by offering to feed union members free as long as the strike lasted. For this they created a hefty sandwich using loaves of French bread. As one legend goes, whenever a union member came through the door, the Martins would say, "Here comes another poor boy!"

In his "Dictionary of American Food and Drink" John Mariani suggests instead that the term is related to the French word for a gratuity, "pourboire" and that the term "poor boy" for a sandwich dates back to 1875.

This sandwich, made of French bread loaves sliced in half lengthwise, can be filled with such tasty possibilities as ham and cheese, roast beef, cheese, oysters or shrimp. And remember, when New Orleanians order their po-boys dressed, they're not making a fashion statement, that's the term for including mayonnaise, lettuce and tomato.

— PSL

HOT ROAST BEEF PO-BOY

Serves 4

If you are roasting your own beef to make some Po-Boys, a rump roast works well, and should be cooked medium well. Save the pan drippings to make the gravy.

1½ lbs. thinly sliced roast beef
1 cup roast beef gravy
4 10-inch lengths of Po-Boy French bread, sliced lengthwise

Shredded lettuce, romaine or iceberg
Thick ripe tomato slices
Mayonnaise, preferably Homemade Mayonnaise, page 46

In a small saucepan, add the sliced beef to the gravy and simmer, covered, for about 15 minutes or until the beef begins to fall apart. Distribute the beef and gravy on the Po-Boy bread and dress the sandwich with lettuce, tomatoes and mayonnaise. Serve immediately.

ROAST BEEF GRAVY

Pan drippings from roasting the beef
3 cups hot water
Butter, if needed

2 Tbls. flour
1 Tbls. minced garlic
1 tsp. black pepper
Salt to taste

Add the water to the roasting pan and stir it around while scraping up all the little bits of drippings stuck to the bottom, then pour it into a small sauce pan. Bring it to a boil and reduce the liquid to about two cups. Remove the pan from the heat and let it rest awhile, allowing the fat to rise to the surface. Skim off the fat and measure it. If necessary, add enough butter to it to equal 2 tablespoons.

In another small saucepan, heat the fat and add the flour. Stir over a medium high heat to make a dark brown roux. (See roux photo, page 10) Remove the pan from the heat and add the garlic, then carefully stir in the contents of the other saucepan. Bring to a boil, add the black pepper and salt to taste, and simmer for about 20 minutes.

CAJUN SHRIMP PO-BOY

Serves 4

The typical New Orleans shrimp Po-Boy is made of shrimp fried in a corn flour batter. We wanted to offer some sort of seafood sandwich, but since we don't have a deep fat fryer in the restaurant, we were unable to prepare the traditional type. This Po-Boy is not really Cajun at all — in fact the preparation is similar to that of a fajita, with the seasoning giving it some local flavor.

4 Tbls. butter or cooking oil
2 red bell peppers, cut in ¼-inch strips
2 green bell peppers, cut in ¼-inch strips
1 large onion, cut in ¼-inch strips
1½ lbs. boiled, peeled shrimp
½ tsp. black pepper
½ tsp. white pepper
½ tsp. cayenne pepper
½ tsp. thyme
½ tsp. basil
½ tsp. granulated garlic
½ tsp. onion powder
1 tsp. salt
1⅓ cup Creole Sauce, page 56
4 10-inch lengths of Po-Boy French bread, sliced lengthwise

Set a 10 or 12 inch black iron skillet over a high heat. Add the butter or oil, then the red bell pepper, green bell pepper and onion. Cook and stir for about 3 minutes or until wilted. Add the shrimp and the seasonings and toss to mix. Stir in the Creole Sauce, cook and stir for about 2 minutes and distribute the mixture on the Po-Boy bread. Serve immediately.

CAJUN SAUSAGE PO-BOY
Serves 4

4 Tbls. butter or cooking oil
2 red bell peppers, cut in ¼-inch strips
2 green bell peppers, cut in ¼-inch strips
1 large onion, cut in ¼-inch strips
1½ lbs. smoked sausage, sliced into ¼-inch rounds
½ tsp. black pepper
½ tsp. white pepper

½ tsp. cayenne pepper
½ tsp. thyme
½ tsp. basil
½ tsp. granulated garlic
½ tsp. onion powder
1 tsp. salt
1⅓ cup Creole Sauce, page 56
4 10-inch lengths of Po-Boy French bread, sliced lengthwise

Set a 10 or 12 inch black iron skillet over a high heat. Add the butter or oil, then the red bell pepper, green bell pepper and onion. Cook and stir for about 3 minutes or until wilted. Add the sausage and the seasonings and toss to mix. Stir in the Creole Sauce, cook and stir for about 2 minutes and distribute the mixture on the Po-Boy bread. Serve immediately.

DESSERTS

Topping off any meal is dessert. The recipe for a praline sauce calls for our wonderful native pecans and a lot of sugar, one of Louisiana's major crops. About 150 years ago, sugar was to south Louisiana what cotton was to the rest of the south. Audubon Park, covering 250 acres of uptown New Orleans was once the sugar plantation of Jean Étienne Boré, New Orleans' first mayor, and also served as the site of the 1884 World's Fair. Indigenous delicacies such as cane syrup, pralines and even a locally distilled rum owe their origin to the Louisiana sugar industry.

A must recipe for dessert is bread pudding. Just as French bread accompanies a meal, it is also an ingredient for this native dessert. Like a gumbo, there are a variety of ingredients that can go into bread pudding. Different chefs also vary the sauces they use as a topping. As tempting as New Orleans food is, the real challenge is to remember to always save room for dessert.

— PSL

BREAD PUDDING WITH WHISKEY SAUCE

Serves 8

¼ cup butter	Pinch of salt
3 cups milk	½ cup sugar
2 quarts day-old French bread, cut into 1-inch cubes	½ tsp. cinnamon
	½ tsp. nutmeg
½ cup cubed pineapple	1 tsp. vanilla
½ cup raisins	3 large eggs, beaten

The ubiquitous New Orleans restaurant dessert, showing up in various signature versions all over town. Ours is a classic rendition, and a perennial favorite of comfort food lovers.

Combine the milk and butter in a saucepan and heat until the butter is melted. In a large mixing bowl combine the bread, pineapple and raisins and toss to mix. Add the milk and butter mixture, mix, and let it stand for several minutes, allowing the bread to absorb the liquid.

Mix the sugar, salt, cinnamon and nutmeg. Add the vanilla to the beaten eggs, then mix in the sugar and spices. Pour all this over the bread and milk mixture and mix well.

Transfer the pudding to a greased 1½ quart baking pan and bake at 350° for 40 minutes or until golden brown. Serve warm, topped with about 3 table-spoons of Whiskey Sauce.

WHISKEY SAUCE

Makes 1¾ cups

¼ cup butter, softened
2 cups confectioners sugar
1 jigger bourbon

Using an electric mixer, slowly cream the sugar into the butter. Slowly beat in the bourbon.

SOUTHERN PECAN PIE

Serves 8

1	cup granulated sugar	½	cup dark corn syrup
½	tsp. cinnamon	1	tsp. vanilla extract
¼	tsp. nutmeg	1½	cups pecan pieces
¼	tsp. salt	1	Tbls. flour
3	large eggs, beaten	1	9-inch unbaked pastry shell
¼	cup melted butter		

Combine the sugar, cinnamon, nutmeg and salt and set aside. Let the melted butter cool a bit and beat it into the eggs along with the corn syrup and vanilla. Add the sugar mixture to the egg mixture and mix well.

In a separate bowl, combine the flour and pecans and toss to mix. Spread the pecans in the pie shell and bake at 400° for 8 minutes. Pour in the sugar/egg mixture and return the pan to the oven. Reduce the heat to 375° and bake for about 40 minutes or until set. Allow the pie to cool before slicing.

Praline Sundae

Makes 4 cups

1   lb. granulated sugar
1   cup dark corn syrup
½   cup water
½   cup double strength black coffee
2   Tbls. butter
2   cups roasted pecan halves or pieces
    Vanilla ice cream

Just one taste of this dark, sweet and slightly bitter sauce and you are immediately transported to a French Quarter patio on a balmy summer night. Enjoy it for dessert over ice cream or cheesecake, or for a special breakfast as a topping for French Toast or pancakes.

Place the sugar in a large, heavy pot and set it over a medium heat. Stirring often, slowly let the sugar melt and caramelize until dark brown, being careful not to let it burn. Stir in the dark corn syrup. Add the water along with the coffee and butter. Bring the pot to a boil, lower to a simmer and cook, stirring occasionally, for about 30 minutes. Remove the pot from the heat and allow it to cool to room temperature. If the sauce is too thick, add a little water.

Add the roasted pecans shortly before serving so they will maintain their crispness. Without the pecans added, the sauce will keep for several weeks in a covered container. If you choose to refrigerate it, which is unnecessary, be sure to let it get back to room temperature before serving.

To make a sundae, pour ½ cup of praline sauce over a scoop of your favorite vanilla ice cream.

CRÈME CARAMEL

Serves 6

2 cups sugar, divided
¼ tsp. nutmeg
¼ tsp. salt
6 eggs, beaten
3 cups milk, scalded
½ cup heavy cream
1 tsp. vanilla extract

Preheat the oven to 325°. Combine 1 cup of the sugar with the nutmeg and salt in a non-reactive bowl. Add the eggs and mix well. Add the heavy cream and scalded milk, mixing well to dissolve the sugar. Stir in the vanilla. Set aside.

Place six 6-ounce custard cups or ramekins in a baking pan and pour in enough hot tap water to come one inch up the outside of the cups. Set aside.

Place the remaining cup of sugar in a heavy bottomed sauce pan and set it over medium heat. Allow the sugar to slowly caramelize, stirring to prevent burning. When the sugar is totally liquid and an even dark amber in color, place about 1 tablespoon or so in the bottom of each cup, tilting slightly to coat part way up the sides. Fill each cup with the custard mixture and carefully place the pan in the oven. Bake for 45 minutes to an hour, or until a knife inserted in the custard about 1 inch from the side of the cup comes out clean. Allow the custard to cool.

To serve, run a small knife around the edge of each cup, and invert it into a small plate. Remove the cup and serve. May be served either at room temperature or chilled.

There was a time when this dessert appeared on menus all over town. Now, with the popularity of Crème Brûlée, it is much less common. We feature it occasionally as a special, sometimes substituting one cup of the milk with a cup of cold drip coffee for a delicious variation. The slightly bitter caramelized sugar in the bottom of the cup creates a perfectly complementary sauce for the rich custard.

LAGNIAPPE

New Orleans has long been a major port for coffee. The coffee companies based here get their beans from Central and South America. The smell of coffee beans roasting stills exists in certain parts of town, and New Orleans continues to be a coffee drinking city. A traditional recipe that combines locals' love of coffee and spirits is Café Brulot. Made with generous amounts of brandy (why be stingy?), "brulot" means "burnt brandy." The inclusion of cinnamon and cloves make this beverage especially popular during the Christmas holidays. Gumbo Shop offers a special Reveillon menu in December. Reveillon was a meal that was served by the Creoles following Midnight Mass on Christmas Eve. In French, the word is derived from a verb meaning "to wake up" and means "midnight supper." The term, Reveillon, has been revived in recent years on special menus offered by area restaurants during Christmas.

— PSL

CAFÉ BRULOT

Serves 10

1	4-inch long cinnamon stick	6	tsp. sugar
12	whole cloves	8	ounces brandy
	The peel of 2 oranges, cut into thin slivers	2	ounces Orange Curacao
	The peel of two lemons, cut into thin slivers	4	cups hot, strong black coffee 151 proof rum, as needed

Every December we participate in the citywide "Christmas New Orleans Style" celebration, serving a special "Reveillon" menu, in addition to our regular fare. The Reveillon is a traditional Creole Yuletide feast, resurrected and reinterpreted by some of the city's finest restaurants. Ours is offered from December first through Christmas Eve and includes five courses, with Café Brulot as lagniappe. The wonderful aroma of the simmering spices and citrus fill the dining room with Christmas cheer. If you don't have a Brulot pot, use a small chafing dish or a fondue pot.

In a Brulot pot or small round chafing dish set over a low flame, muddle the cinnamon, cloves, citrus peels and sugar with a ladle. Add the brandy and Orange Curacao and mix well. Carefully ignite the mixture and stir until the sugar is dissolved. If you have difficulty lighting it, you can add a little 151 proof rum to help, but be very careful. Slowly pour in the coffee while continuing to stir until the flame dies out. Serve in brulot cups or demitasse cups.

SAZERAC COCKTAIL

½ tsp. Herbsaint Liqueur
2 ounces rye whiskey
½ ounce simple syrup

3 drops Peychaud's Bitters
   Twist of lemon peel

Pour Herbsaint Liqueur into a 9 ounce rocks glass and swirl or toss to coat sides of glass.

Pour rye whiskey, simple syrup and Peychaud's Bitters over ice in a mixing glass. Stir until chilled and strain into rocks glass over two ice cubes. Rub lemon peel around the rim of the glass and add to drink.

BOURBON MILK PUNCH

2 ounces bourbon
1 ounce simple syrup
3 ounces milk

¼ tsp. pure vanilla extract
   Freshly grated nutmeg

Pour all ingredients over ice in a metal shaker. Shake vigorously until well chilled and frothy. Strain over ice into a 12 ounce tall glass. Sprinkle with nutmeg. Substitute bourbon with brandy for a variation.

Some time around 1795 the French Dominican Pharmacist Antoine Peychaud migrated to Louisiana and set up shop in La Nouvelle Orleans. His apothecary produced a signature bitters which still bears his name. He combined a bit of the bitters with some Sazerac de Forge Cognac, a little sugar and, serving the concoction in an egg cup, or "coquetier," reputedly created the world's first cocktail. Eventually, rye whiskey replaced the cognac and the drink was served in an Absinthe laced glass. The popularity of the cocktail resulted in a succession of Sazerac bars in the city, including the elegant watering hole still operating in the lobby of the New Orleans Fairmont Hotel.

Ramos Gin Fizz

Created by Henry Ramos in his downtown bar sometime during the 1880's, it is the egg white and orange flower (a French perfume) that distinguish this gin fizz from others. A wonderful springtime brunch starter, it should be drunk quickly, least the fizz fizzle.

2	ounces gin	1	egg white
1	ounce simple syrup	2	ounces milk
½	ounce fresh lemon juice	6-8	drops orange flower water

Pour all ingredients over ice in a metal shaker. Shake vigorously (at least 100 times) until your hand sticks to the container. Strain over ice into a 12 ounce tall glass. Float an additional 3 to 4 drops of orange flower water on top of the drink if desired.

Mint Julep

2	ounces bourbon	6-8	fresh mint leaves
1	ounce simple syrup		Crushed ice

Muddle mint leaves and simple syrup in the bottom of a tall glass. Fill glass with crushed ice. Pour bourbon over ice and stir. Garnish with a sprig of fresh mint.

HONEYDEW DAIQUIRI

2 ounces Ron Rico Gold Rum
2 ounces Midori melon liqueur
4 ounces fresh honeydew
   melon

1 ounce simple syrup
1 ounce fresh lemon juice
  Slice of fresh honeydew
   melon

Pour all ingredients into blender container over ice. Blend for 30 seconds and pour into a 16 ounce glass. Garnish with a slice of fresh honeydew.

During the notoriously hot and humid summer months orders for our individually made fresh fruit daiquiris keep the bartenders quite busy. This one's unique and particularly refreshing.

ST. PETER'S PUNCH

2 ounces Ron Rico Gold Rum
1 ounce Sloe Gin
6 ounces pineapple juice

Slice of fresh orange
Maraschino cherries

Pour ingredients over ice in metal shaker. Shake until thoroughly chilled. Pour into a 16 ounce glass and garnish with an orange slice and red Maraschino cherries.

GLOSSARY
and other important ingredient information

ANDOUILLE: A smoky, peppery, heavily smoked pork sausage of Cajun origin, usually thicker in diameter than other smoked sausages. Pronounced "an-dewey."

BOUDIN: A fresh pale colored Cajun sausage made with various parts of pork, lots of seasoning and rice. Boudin is usually boiled and eaten out of hand. We grill ours and serve it with Creole mustard. Pronounced "boo-dan."

CRAWFISH: A freshwater crustacean that looks like a tiny lobster. Sometimes referred to as mudbugs, crawfish are popular and plentiful in Louisiana. Crawfish are available live, boiled whole, or as peeled tails packed in one pound packages. For years Louisiana produced about 95% of the world crawfish supply. The increased popularity of Creole and Cajun food has created a burgeoning crawfish industry in the far east, with Chinese peeled tails now widely available. We recommend using only fresh tail meat, as the frozen versions often lack flavor and are of inferior texture.

CREOLE MUSTARD: This staple of every corner Po-Boy shop in New Orleans is also an essential ingredient in remoulade sauce. Prepared from only brown mustard seeds, vinegar and salt, the best quality is Zatarain's.

ETOUFFEE: Derived from the French verb meaning "to smother," in this case describes a cooking method in which crawfish, shrimp or sometimes other ingredients are smothered in a spicy sauce containing lots of onions. Pronounced "a-too-fay."

FILÉ: This contribution to Louisiana cuisine came from the indigenous Choctaw Indians. It is the ground leaves of the sassafras tree and is used as a unique flavoring and thickening agent in some gumbo recipes. Pronounced "fee-lay."

GUMBO: Although the word defies a concise definition, to a native it is perfectly clear what is, or is not, gumbo. While akin to soup, stew and bouillabaisse, gumbo constitutes a category all its own. Okra, filé and roux all play important roles, but never all in the same pot. The common threads are sautéed seasoning vegetables including onion, bell pepper and, usually celery and garlic, and a rich stock. Enjoy gumbo in small portions as a hearty first course or in soup bowls as a one dish meal.

HERBSAINT: A locally produced licorice flavored liqueur used in place of Absinthe as an ingredient in cocktails and some recipes. Pronounced "erbsaint."

JAMBALAYA: Similar in appearance and texture to paella, but differing in ingredients and method of preparation. The origin of this dish, both the recipe and the name, is the subject of vigorous debate among some of the ethnic groups that have contributed to our culinary heritage.

LAGNAIPPE: A French word meaning something extra or free of charge, or some added value — similar in concept to a baker's dozen. Pronounced "lan-yap."

OKRA: A green pod vegetable, filled with soft edible seeds. Okra is native to Africa and grows abundantly well throughout the southern United States. It is a very common ingredient in New Orleans style gumbo, adding flavor, texture and substance, but rarely found in a Cajun gumbo. Okra is also enjoyed locally as a side dish, usually stewed with tomatoes.

REDFISH: A saltwater fish of the drum family, with a reddish tint to the scales and a round black spot on the tail fin. Black drum is a perfectly fine substitute, but avoid the "bull drums" or "bull reds" (fillets over twelve ounces) as they tend to be tough.

ROUX: Basically flour browned in some sort of fat, and an essential ingredient in many Louisiana dishes. See page 10 for very detailed instructions on how to make a roux. Pronounced "roo."

TASSO: Sometimes referred to as Cajun bacon, tasso is made from pickled pork that has been rubbed with a peppery spice mixture, air dried and then smoked. The flavor is intense and it is used sparingly as a seasoning for a variety of dishes. Pronounced "tasso."

SOURCES

NEW ORLEANS FISH HOUSE
921 South Dupre Street
New Orleans, LA 70125
800-839-3474
504-821-9700
www.nofh.com
Full line of fresh and frozen fish, shrimp, crabmeat, alligator meat, crawfish, smoked seafood, sausage, andouille and tasso.

BATTISTELLA'S SEA FOODS, INC.
910 Touro Street
New Orleans, LA 70116
800-375-2728
504-949-2724
504-949-2799 FAX
batpak@bellsouth.net
Fresh and frozen fish, crawfish, crabmeat, shrimp and oysters.

CRESCENT CITY MEATS
7133 Ivy Street
Metairie, LA 70003
800-375-1956
504-737-0570
Sausage, andouille, tasso, boudin, alligator sausage.

PAP'S LOUISIANA CUISINE, INC.
16322 Highway 929
Prairieville, LA 70769
225-622-3262
paps@intersurf.com
Sausage, andouille, tasso, boudin.

ZATARAIN
P. O. Box 347
Gretna, LA 70053
504-367-2950
www.zatarain.com
Creole mustard, crab boil, spices, mixes.

GUMBO SHOP
Catering Department
5900 South Front Street
New Orleans, LA 70115
800-554-8626
504-899-2460
www.gumboshop.com
Prepared New Orleans gumbos, soups, sauces and entrées shipped nationwide. Gumbo Shop cookbooks, tee shirts and hats.

INDEX

RESTAURANT
630 Saint Peter Street
New Orleans, LA 70116
504-525-1486
fax 504-524-0747

OFFICE and CATERING
5900 South Front Street
New Orleans, LA 70115
504-899-2460
fax 504-897-3454
800-55GUMBO
www.gumboshop.com